A BEGINNER'S GUIDE TO DAY TRADING

HOW TO MAKE PROFIT WITH SHORT-TERM TRADING. STOCKS, MASTER ETFS, FUTURES AND FOREX THROUGH THE STRATEGIES OF THE BEST TRADERS

Andrew Hunter

Table of Contents

Introduction

Day trading is one of, if not the most difficult things you will undertake inyour life. So, having to practice shouldn't come as a surprise. Below, I will cover the ten reasons why you should practice day trading.

Day Trading is super-fast

Talk about knocking it down first in the post, but the daily trade is very fast. I've done everything from swing trading, long-term investing, and day trading, and by far day trading requires a unique set of skills. If you think about chess, what is one way you can increase the chess difficulty level? Puta stopwatch on how long you need to make a move. This is where real skill emerges because intuition, experience, and repetition come into play. Well, the market is no different. If I have a few days to analyze a position, I can work out a good trading plan with notes for myself. When operating during the day, it can only take a few minutes to a few seconds to make a decision. So, you think chess players start playing with a 1-minute timer? Obviously not. Therefore, you shouldn't even end up on the market with your hard-earned money, trying to make some harmless transactions. Take time to practice day trading to develop the skills necessary to enter the field.

Practice day trading in response to the market

The market is a real living being. While you have a history of some price movements, each day is unique. You'll have to see how you react to it when the tape airs and the actions move. It's one thing to just look at the old charts, but you have to get used to listening to the market. Much of day trade is intuition. This is the part of your trading toolbox that you cannot quantify andit is unique to you and your trading style. This will permit you to learn how stocks react when the market generally makes sudden movements in both directions.

Learn to manage your money

One thing I say is that I cannot practice day trading on a simulatorbecause it is not real money. To some extent, this is true. But if there was a fire, did you know where to go? Did you know what path you should follow to get out of the building? Did your teachers know how long it would take to get all the children out? Did the firefighter expect where to be within a certainperiod of time?

This is why you need to learn to manage your money. You have to get used to calculate the gains and losses in your head. You must learn to trade effectively on margin. Risk compensation ratios must be evaluated quickly and only the best opportunities should be run, as there are five to choose fromat the same time. Now, you can read this and say, well, it's not real moneyyet, so I'm not going to take it seriously, and you know what, you reserve the right to make that adult decision. But for me personally, I always want to know what to do in case of fire.

Find out how to manage winning and losing trades

Trading is excellent when you are making money. The beauty of being in this losing position is that it quickly humiliated me in a matter of days. The critical thing I know and will learn to develop over time is that you must forget the losers and winners the moment you close your position. Bringing your personal grudges to the next operation will only harm you because there are new market participants in every action. Therefore, practicing trade allows you to speed up the pace. When I say rhythm, I mean the negotiation cycle. Some win, others lose, but you must learn to deal with every trade witha positive mindset and sound trading principles. This is another one of those skill sets that come from pure repetition. You just have to make a horrible trade just to follow 15 direct winners to realize that the lousy trade doesn't require you to start psychoanalyzing your infancy.

You need your 10,000 hours of practice

I know, I know, so, I'll keep it short. Studies have shown that you need to practice something for 10,000 hours before you become an expert. Think about your personal jobs or careers. If you are an executive, employersrequire 10 to 15 years of job search experience. If you do simple math, a full-time equivalent per year is 2.00 hours. So, if you really think about it,employers are saying you should have 20,000 to 30,000 hours of experience before allowing you to run a department. Well, guess what; The same is true for day trading. Overtime training will allow you to exponentially increasethe time required to reach that 10,000 hours expert level.

Know that all charts don't go to the moon

Earlier in my career, I would have scoured the market for specific configurations that would have made significant profits. I would identify a particular model with the same indicators to find that weak point. Afterconfiguring my settings, historically, these winning rankings seemed to be everywhere. The problem was that when I tried to do it in real-time, things didn't work as expected. Day trading today is done with computers and the level of ongoing games in terms of fake breakouts is insane. What taught me to practice day trading is that it is more important to reserve the earnings of singles than to always swing by the fences. These take me to the moon setting; they will only pay 10% to 20% of the time, so stop waiting for it to happen every time you trade. Focus on the rhythm of just winning and when the big trade comes, you'll know it.

Discover your day trading style

Personally, I believe that as adults, we are responsible for our decisions inlife. Don't blame your parents or some events that happened to you in third grade for why you do certain things in your life. I'm not trying to rule out the impact of life experiences, but what I'm saying is that we can choose how long we let them influence how we live our lives. Well, for day trading, I think, for the most part, it's easier not to "take over" your trading strategy andleave it to the expert. Most people will go in and fight to put together a system: paralysis analysis at its best. So, go to Google, do some searchingand voila, there is your friendly "day trade expert" ready to sell you the magic keys to your promise land. I am not judging you; I have spent thousands on other people's courses, hoping to find myself. What I realized isthat these courses are other people's rules. Trading requires that you understand what works for you. Guess what, people, it's work. It will literally take thousands of hours to modify and re-optimize to understand what corresponds to your business DNA. The reason I chose to go my way was when these systems started to fail, who did I start blaming? You guessed it right, the man behind the curtain who sold me this excellent course. Please dome a favor and skip all this pain. I'm not saying that you can't collectfundamental principles from other day traders, but you have to define your methodology yourself. Only you can do it, so when things go wrong, you don't blame mom or dad, you look in the mirror.

You need more reps

If you've ever tried for a sports team, practices are only for a certain period of time each day. Therefore, you only have a limited window to show your coach that you have what it takes to be a team member. Since we only exchange buds in the morning, I have a maximum of 2-4 exchanges that I cando on any given day. It would take me a little over 2 months to have 100 trades to analyze.

Show Yourself You can be a day trader

Market research is none other than Monday's quarterback. You start totell yourself; I would have been in that trade and would have made this sum of money. But you are looking back on the old lists of things that havealready been played; however, in a market simulation environment, there is tremendous value to you, with real data that you have everything you need to make money. At the end of the day, you must believe that regardless of your background, education or age, you can do it. If you practice day trading long enough, you will get to that point where you can tell yourself that I am a professional day trader.

See how long you can expect to do daily operations

What better way to see it yourself than to go to a simulator and start the account balance with the money at hand. Depending on your system and how long you have it, it can take a few weeks or months to swap a full calendar year. At the end of the year, after considering fees and living expenses, how much money do you have left? Practicing day trading can begin to answer some of these confusing aspects of day trading.

What is Financial Trading?

Like any other investment that you can take part in, day trading is designed to earn you a profit at the end of the day. You can turn it into a successful career that you can use to sustain your livelihood. There are some heated debates among different individuals, with concerns if you can generatea sustainable income from trading. Well, I would say that it is possible since we already have individuals that are literally living from it. I think how we choose to trade has a significant impact on the results that we get at the endof the trade. One of the most significant factors contributing to trading success is having the right information. Take time to get the information rightfrom the beginning. You might have started your trading career recently. But your willingness to learn sets you apart from the rest. Like any journey, the goal is to get to the destination. Your mode of transport may vary, and it will bring a difference in the time you will arrive and the comfort that you willget. The same applies to day trading. Some people easily earn from it, and at the same time, there are those who have many regrets that they engaged inthe trade in the first place. Choose the path that you wish to take as you start your trading career. The years of experience may not matter, but the determination that you have to learn more will get you far.

The strategies that you decide to settle for will determine the outcome of the majority of the trades that you make. As a good trader, you need to have a good trading plan that will help you while trading. Now, you will comeacross some tips that will make your trading career worth your while. You need to be open to the challenges that you will encounter as a trader. Thereare some risks that will expose your trade to the potential of suffering a loss, and you need to be open to the whole idea. At the same time, you need to be familiar with the different risk management plans that you can engage in to ensure that you have an easy time managing the risks that you come across. Trading is not an easy venture that you get to joy-ride in and still walk away with profits. The efforts that you make in getting better at trading will set youapart and ensure that you become a better trader. There are some moments that you will feel proud of the decisions that you made, and other times, you will wish that you never made those decisions. You have to be okay with the idea that you may get a loss or a profit. I have outlined some of the tips that you can use to ensure your trading success. With the right plan and strategy, you will make a living out of day trading.

Day trading is a profitable investment, and there is a lot that you canmake as a trader. The different trading strategies and trading plan will help you stay on top of your game as a trader. In the book, I have tried to provide information that will help you become a better trader. I will not promise thatit will be an easy journey. The steps that you take toward becoming a better trader will set you apart despite the bumps that you will come across. Anybody can make a good trade as long as they have the right attitude.

Advanced Tools for

The Day Trader

Ever come across this saying that a day trader is only as fine as the tools they are working with? We shall take a look at the different tools used in day trading.

Best Software for Day Trading.

A day trading software is a term given to any software that can help in thedecision making and analysis in order to make a trade. Some of the software will provide you with accessibility to the tools and all the resources needed.

A day trading software has the following basic features:

- Any software should have the functionality of allowing the setup oftrading strategy in the system.
- Possess the order-placing function which is normally automated.
- Tools for continuous assessment of the market developments so as to acton them.

Zacks Trade

The pros of this software are that:

• It is quite rare to find a trading platform that offers cheap commission such as a cent. To engage in trading the penny stocks, you will need to pay around 1% of the trade's value with a minimum cost of $3. The cost for options is around $3 for the first contract and cost of additional ones which is75 cents.

• Zacks normally offers investors with the accessibility to 26 research and 87 reports on subscriptions.

• This software is also available for Linux users. Account-holders can alsoaccess Zacks using their mobile phones unlike it is seen on other software.

• Zacks Trade is so safe and secure. Clients normally have their own platforms from the management and they register for their accounts with unique usernames and passwords.

• Good customer service. This

platform enables day traders who use their smartphones to trade for a free 24/7-hour basis. It is mostly for traders suited in Asia, the US, and Australia.

The shortcoming for this software is that it offers slightly higher charges on shares as compared to Interactive brokers.

Interactive Brokers.

This software is strongly advisable for advanced and frequent traders. It charges $0.01 per share with no minimum investment required. It offers a wide range of investments such as European bonds for the government and the corporate. Interactive brokers offer research for free to its traders from around 100 providers such as Zacks and many more.
The advantages of this software include:

- The low commission charges on exchange-traded funds and stock tend tofavor the frequent traders. The low rates also favor the margin traders.

- Interactive Broker's workstation is fast and offers great features such as watchlists, real-time monitoring, and advanced charting.

- Another great advantage of Interactive Broker is that it offers its traders massive accessibility to research and news services which keeps them up to date.

The greatest shortcoming of Interactive Brokers is that traders find it hardto navigate through the website. This makes it difficult for traders to identify the costs associated with the commissions and fees.

TD Ameritrade.

This is one of the largest trading brokerage software with the basic and Thinkorswim platforms. It charges fees of $6.95 per share and no minimum investment is required. The Thinkorswim platform allows clients tocustomize color schemes and layouts according to their choice of preference. Trade tickets are found on both of the platforms so a trader can enter an orderin whichever platform you are using.

After the software development team made updates on the tools andcontent of this software, there has been an improved look on both of the platforms making it more responsive to the client's devices.

TD Ameritrade offers a range of tradable

securities; over 300 exchange- traded funds are free of charge and over 12,000 mutual funds. It also provides investors and traders accessibility to research for good quality trade executionespecially for traders using the Thinkorswim platform.
Trade Station.

Trade Station is a day training software that charges $5 per share and requires a minimum investment of $500. It normally focuses on good quality data of the market and the trade executions. Its system is well established andnormally remains firm during market surges. You can establish your own system using the analysis tools and mock testing strategies provided by this software.

The advantages of this software are as follows:

- The platform has minimal chances of crashing down since it is a stable platform.

- The software feature out excellent charting tools and back testing strategies making it the popular software.

- Education support for this software is at top-notch. It normally offers classes and educational videos to its traders on various topics such as margins and many others.

The shortcoming of this software is that there no cases of forex tradingand international trading is limited.

eOption

eOption is another day trading software that focuses on quality. It has a minimum investment of $500 and charges $3 per trade. The massive number of fans of option is mostly after the low commission and the extreme faster trade executions.

You can check out the platform before opening the account by using Paper Trading Toolset which is given for free for around 45 days.

This software has various pros:

It is easy for traders to navigate through the web-based platform. The user interface is so simple and the tools provided are easier to be found by thetraders.

- Good customer service. The platform is so stable and seldom has casesof crashing down.
- The cost of using this software is very low since the charge per trade is $3.

- However, users for inactive accounts are normally charged an annual fee of $50.

The cons of this software are:

- Limited accessibility for the traders to research and news providersunlike in other software.

- Education support is not that good. The offerings are limited making it difficult for new traders.

Firs trade.

This is a trading software which is free of charge and requires a minimum investment of $0. It began offering $0 commission to traders dealing with options and the stock recently and for its benefit, it offered limited tools and research for the traders using this software. Firs trade also has this lending program which provides lending services to financial bodies and account holders and they can generate income. The traders can even sell the stockwith no restrictions.

Some of the pros of this software include the following:

- It provides a set of accounts. It has

simplified English, traditional andeven Chinese accounts.

- •It has lower costs. Charges $0 for the stock and options traders.
- •This software provides access to stocks, options and funds type oftrading. The drawbacks of this software include the following:
- •Firs trade does not provide access to forex, future and crypto type of trading.
- •It does not have a 24/7 basis for customer support. They only operate in limited hours as compared to other brokerage trading platforms.
- •This platform has a few functionalities for its traders. Its traders areforced to use functionality from other platforms.

Trading View.

This is a trading software that is free, also has monthly charges of $9.95 for the Pro account, $19.95

for the Pro+ account and $39.95 for the premium account. Trading View does not support stock options and U.S trading.

A trader can make trades on the charts and the software will work out for you the profit and loss reports and analysis.

Its advantages include the following:

•This software is of ease of use even to beginners.

•Offer support for a variety of trades such as stock, forex, andcryptocurrency.

•The charting for this software is easy to use and provides you with various tools.

The disadvantage of this software that turns many off is that it has noreal-time news for the traders, unlike other trading software.

Tools and Services Used for Day Trading

For an effective job in day trading, a trader is required to possess a set of tools and services. Some of the tools required are the basic ones that you already possess such as a laptop or computer and a telephone.

Other tools that a trader may need include a charting platform and also real-time data. The tools and services needed by a day trader to be on the move include the following:Laptop or computer.

Technology nowadays keeps on changing rapidly. A trader should at leastpossess a good laptop or computer with excellent memory and processors. A good computer processor will speed up the trade executions for excellent trade results. Also, a machine with high memory will have the capability of backing up the market data and there will be minimal chances of the computer crashing down.

Charting software.

Day trading software provided by companies or outside vendors normallyhave different features. Some software has charting platforms where traders can keep track of the price changes of the stock. Price charts make work easier for traders making their work effective and efficient. Software that lacks charting platforms makes it tough for new traders making contributing to slow trades. A day trader should mostly prefer software with charting platforms.

Internet.

Internet is one of the crucial resources required by online users. The Internet with fast speed produces effective work. A trader is able to be up-to- date with the current prices in the market. Workflow also becomes smooth since there is no lagging behind web pages unlike it is seen on slow internet. A trader should, of course, set high priorities for service providers with good internet speeds for excellent works.

Telephone.

In case you need to cut down the costs of the internet, a trader is advised to possess a cell phone or a landline. A telephone will assist you in contactingyour broker in case your offline. You will need to back up the broker's contact number on your telephone for assistance.

Real-time market data.

Market data constitute of prices and markets you choose to trade. The market can be futures, options, forex, and even stocks. It is upon you as a trader to decide on the type of market you want and contacts your broker. Some brokers offer all the market data for free but with high commission.

Broker.

A day trading broker can be a company or small brokers. A brokerprovides a trader with the necessary market trades according to your choiceof preference. Different brokers provide software with different features.

Some may include platforms with all trade's others with limited trades.Software with all trades most times requires payment of high commission ending up being a big burden for the inactive and small traders. It is mostly advisable to select smaller but regulated brokers who provide lower commissions.

Charts

Types of Charts

Technical analysis is the study of price, volume, and time to identify patterns that have happened in the past and that might repeat again in the future. Technical analysts (sometimes called technicians) have many tools available to them today, and one of the most basic is the chart. Day traders can find charts from a variety of sources and service providers.

Line Chart

A chart plots price on the vertical y axis and time on the horizontal x axis. The right side of the chart represents the most recent data, and beyond that, there is nothing—it is the future. The line chart is the simplest type of price chart. It can be plotted for any time frame, such as intraday (5, 10, 20 minutes), hourly, daily, weekly, or monthly.

For example, a simple line chart for EUR/USD is plotted below. It is a daily chart, meaning the chart updates with each new trading day, and the most recent trading day is on the far right. The euro has not performed well against the dollar during this period, and this daily line chart shows a notable decline, or downtrend. Time to book that dream trip to the Amalfi coast you've always dreamed about.

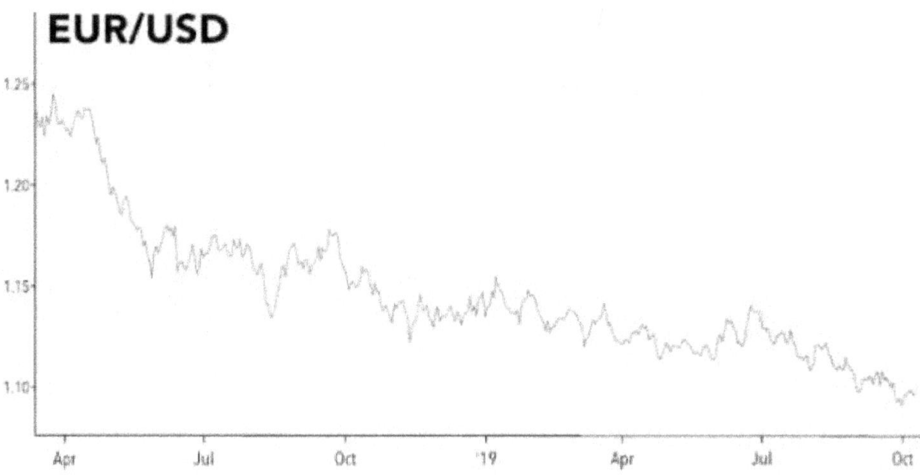

Bar Charts

Line charts plot only the most recent (last or closing) price, but bar charts include several other pieces of price information. These charts are sometimes called OHLC charts—for Open, High, Low, Close—and they capture fourdifferent prices of the day (or of any time frame selected).

Open: This is the first price within the period defined by the bar, and is asmall horizontal line on the left side of the bar.

High: The top of the bar is the highest price of the day.

Low: The lowest point on the bar is the lowest price of the day.

OHLC CHART

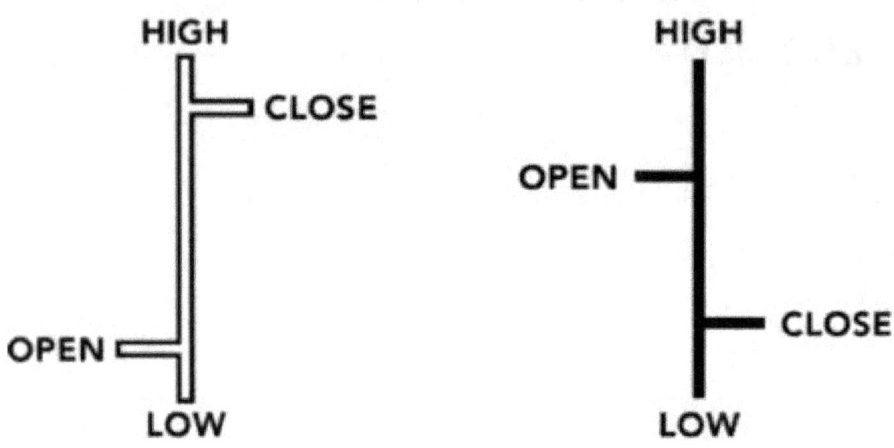

Close: The final or last price of the day (or the most recent price if themarket is open) is the little horizontal line on the right side of the bar.

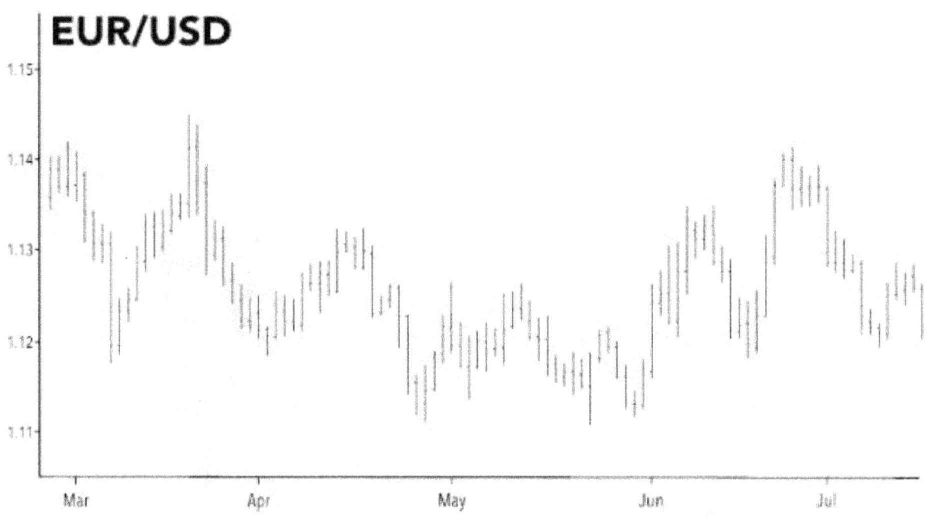

Since each bar captures the high and low price, its length gives us a sense of the range of price movement. Longer bars reveal that the trading range (difference between high and low) is greater than in periods when the bars areshorter in length. The picture above shows the OHLC for the EUR/USD currency pair over a period of several months.

Candlestick Charts

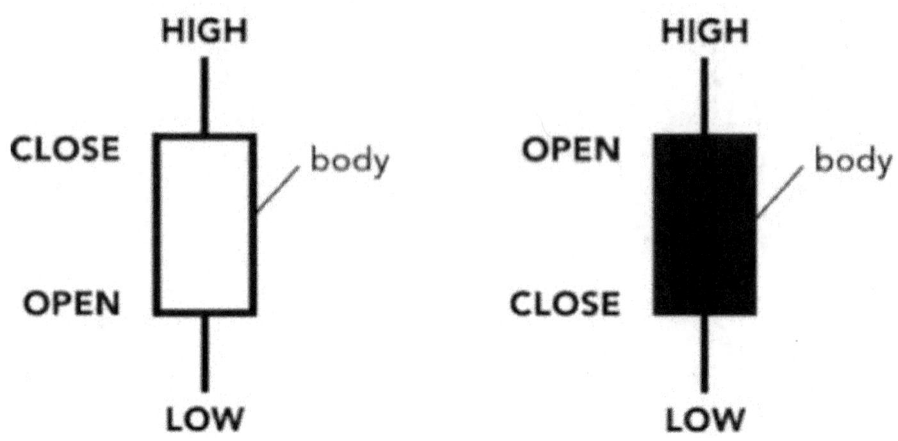

Many examples you can find on the web use candlestick charts, which arecenturies-old tools first used by Japanese rice farmers. A daily candlestick chart captures the open, high, low, and close prices of the day. The main difference between a bar chart and a candlestick chart is that there is a rectangular "body" on the candlestick created by the open and close of the bar.

The lines above and below the body on a candlestick bar, which look like candle wicks, represent the highs and lows of the bar. The length of each candlestick will vary based on the bar's highs and lows, and the body will be bigger or smaller depending on the difference between the open and close prices, with a large body indicating a wider range between the first price and the last price of the bar.

Also, the color of the bar matters. Red (or dark, in black and white charts)on a daily chart means the market opened higher and closed lower—it was a down day (or down bar). Green (or lighter color) suggests the market closed higher than where it opened—it was an up day (or up bar). In other words, candlestick charts typically use lighter colors, like green; to indicate that the bar closed higher than where it opened. Darker colors like red are used to indicate the opposite.

Like line charts, bar and candlestick charts can be plotted for any time frame. Daily charts are the most common, with each bar representing one trading day. Weekly and monthly charts give a glimpse of longer-term trends.Day traders usually focus on short-term charts. In some charts each barrepresents 5, 10, 15, or some other amount of minutes of data. In other charts,each bar represents a certain number of ticks, such as 233, 377, or 610 ticks. Another type of chart has bars that represent the spanning of a particular pricerange.

The main reason I rely on candlestick charts, and why you will see them used throughout the book, is that I find them more visually appealing thanline or bar charts. Also, candlesticks reveal a lot of useful information about price changes. They are easy on the eyes and quite simple to understand once you get the basics. I also use OHLC charts for day trading at times, because you can fit far more price bars on OHLC charts than on candlestick charts, which gives you a larger and longer-term perspective.

Day Trading Chart Types

Some of the best charts for day trading are based on ranges, number of ticks, or volume. These charts are a bit different than the traditional price charts, which merely plot price over time. Let's look at six examples of short-term charts of the Russell E-mini to better understand what kind of charts ideal for day are trading.

Time-Based Charts

We have already looked at examples of daily time-based charts, but day traders typically want to focus on intraday charts with intervals like two, five,or 10 minutes. For instance, is a two-minute chart, which simply means that after two minutes a bar closes and a new one opens? The concept is the same as with a daily or weekly chart, but the time interval is only two minutes.

I call this a fast-time-frame chart (as opposed to a daily chart, which would bea slower chart). It is a perfect tool for watching price action and trading different setups intraday.

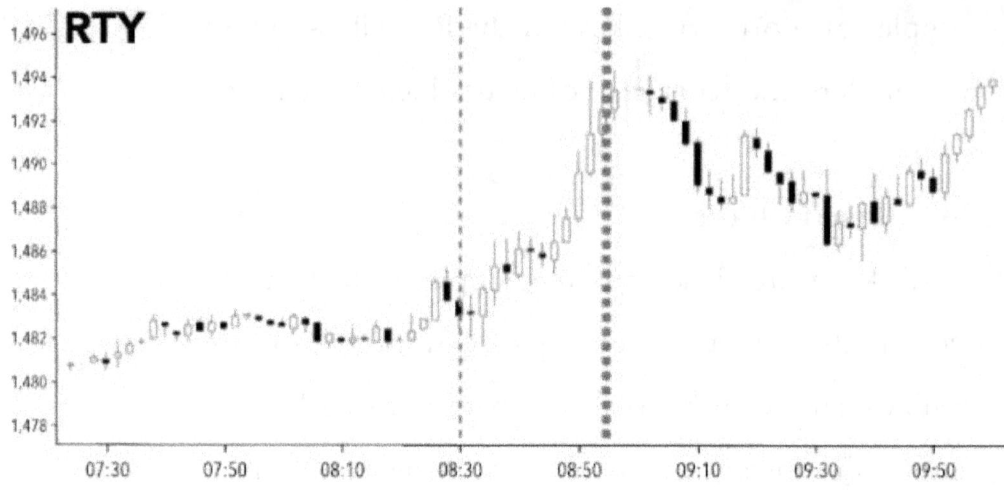

RTY
1,496
1,494
1,492
1,490
1,488
1,486
1,484
1,482
1,480
1,478
07:30
07:50
08:10
08:30
08:50
09:10
09:30
09:50

The vertical lines on this two-minute chart of the Russell E-mini (RTY) denote about 25 minutes ($\approx$12 bars) of activity between 8:30 and 8:54 a.m. For purposes of comparison, a similar time demarcation has been made on several of the other charts featured.

Tick Charts

A tick chart does not consider time. Instead, the chart updates based onthe number of ticks traded for a given instrument. The simplest example is a one-tick chart, which updates with every trade. On the other hand, is a 377- tick candlestick chart. Therefore, it updates after 377 trades have occurred. Inan active market, 377 ticks can happen in seconds, but in a slow market it canseem like a lifetime. Since I trade only the most active and liquid markets, I really like charts like this—233, 377, or 610 ticks—because I can get a better sense of how fast or slow the market is moving.

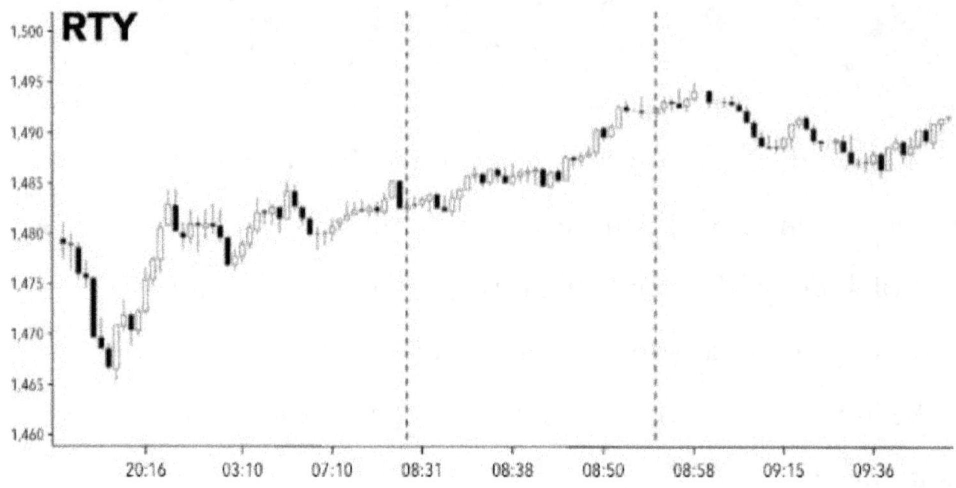

RTY
1,500
1,495
1,490
1,485
1,480
1,475
1,470
1,465
1,460
20:16
03:10
07:10
08:31
08:38
08:50
08:58
09:15
09:36

Momentum Range Bar Charts

The momentum range bar chart, or momentum bar chart, is one of severaltypes of range bar charts that we will introduce. Range bar charts are unique in that price action (rather than time) determines when the next bar is addedto the chart. A range bar chart plots a new bar each time a specified range of price action (8 ticks, for instance) occurs. Every bar on the chart would be 8 ticks, from high to low (or low to high).

Unless you want to experience demoralizing frustration, don't go out and try this approach until you have at least finished reading and studying this book. As I've said before, nothing is ever perfect in trading, and various stepstaken by traders, such as the use of momentum bar charts, require practiceand becoming familiar with how these charts work.

Range bars are very dynamic because they only consider price range, and we make our living by trading price action. For that reason, range bar charts are one of my favorite chart types. They can be tricky to understand at first, because the chart's horizontal axis does not correlate with time and we arenot accustomed to that. Range bar charts can move fast, slow, or somewhere in between. I typically choose charts that move at a pace that suits my trading approach.

Notice that, in our momentum range bar chart if you include the wicks, allthe candlesticks are the same length from high to low. Each bar is created when the price achieves a specified range, so the uniform length of each bar reflects that range. Notice also how each new bar opens either 1 tick above or1 tick below the prior bar. In a normal range bar chart, you would see the price of each bar open on (at the same price as) the high or low of the priorbar.

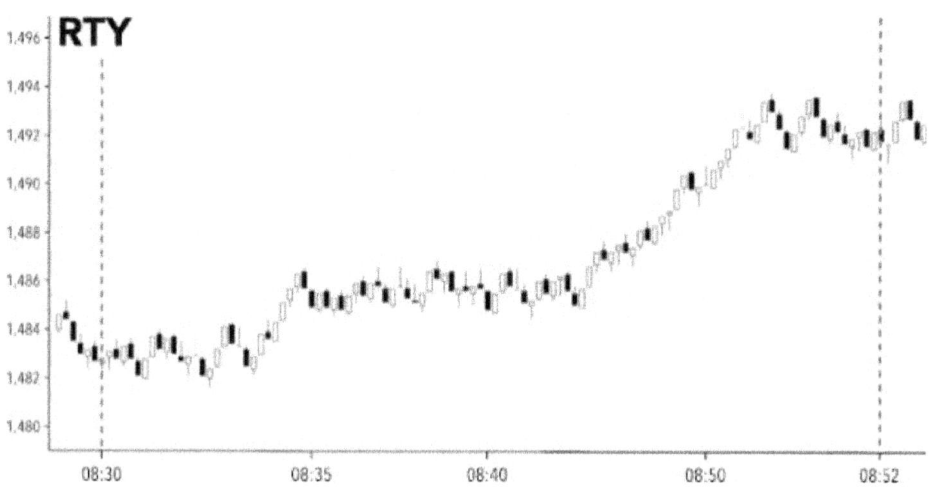

Some charting platforms, such as TradeStation, allow you to choosebetween a momentum bar chart and a standard range bar chart. Other platforms offer only one or the other.

Some charting platforms allow access only to momentum bars, but they refer to them simply as "range bars." Since you now know the difference between the two, you should be able to easily distinguish them when youlook at a chart. Just ask yourself, "Does the new bar open on the closing high or low of the prior bar (range bar) or does it open one tick beyond the high or low of the prior bar (momentum bar)?"

Renko Bars

The Renko bar is another type of range bar chart. The word "renga" means brick in Japanese, and, given that the Renko chart has Japanese origins, it's commonly believed that the word "Renko" is derived from the word "renga."

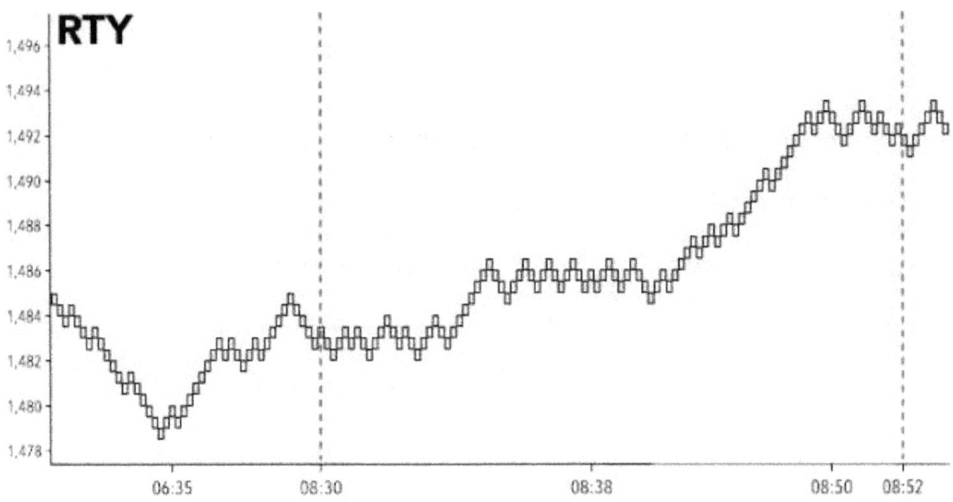

The chart's unique appearance is its defining feature, with each bar resembling a brick. Otherwise it behaves just like a standard range bar chart with each bar opening exactly on the high or low of the previous bar.

We see the price action in the Russell E-mini. All the Renko bars are the same size, equal to a 5 tick. Each brick must achieve the 5 ticks of range either above or below the prior bar in order to close.

Price points are reached beyond each bar that we will never know about, as they will not show up on the standard Renko chart. The price must travel the range of the bar for the bar to close. For example, the current price could move 4 ticks higher than the previously closed Renko bar, then move 2 ticks lower than the low of the prior bar, then back up again, back down again, etc.Not until the bar moves 5 ticks above or below the prior bar will the current bar close, beginning the same process all over again. We would never know where the price had traveled prior to the bar closing. We only know that inthe end it either moved up 5 ticks or down 5 ticks to finally close that bar. Mean Renko and custom Renko bars do show you these unseen price points, as they have wicks attached to the bar.

The Technical Analysis

There are two types of methods used by professional day traders toanalyze trades and help them in making investment decisions. These are technical analysis and fundamental analysis. The fundamental analysis involves studying the basic nature of a company to make a projection of its value. On the other hand, Technical Analysis follows a completely distinct method: it does not take into account the value of the company and will only look into the movements of the price in the market.

In spite of all the remarkable tools used in Technical Analysis, it is really all about looking into the current supply and demand in the stock market, to determine what trend or direction will happen in the future. This style of analysis will allow you to understand the emotional factor in the market by looking into the market as a whole and not the individual movements. Understanding the advantages and restrictions of technical analysis can provide you with new set of tools as well as skills, which will allow you to become a better day trader.

You will learn the fundamental concepts of technical analysis. It is quite abroad subject, which is worthy of another book, so we will just discuss the basics to provide you with the foundation you need so you will be able to make sense of more advanced topics as you go on with day trading.

Technical Analysis - The Basics

Technical Analysis refers to the strategy of studying stocks by looking into the statistics representing the market activity such as the stock volume and past prices. In technical analysis, you don't have to make sense of the company's intrinsic value. You have to make sense of charts and use advanced tools so you can detect patterns that may continue in the nearfuture.

There are different kinds of technical analysis. Some require the use of chart patterns, others depend on oscillators and technical indicators, while most use a mixture of these styles. Nonetheless, technical analysis is characterized by the exclusive use of historical price and volume information,which makes it distinctive from fundamental analysis.

Not similar to fundamental analysis, technical analysts do not really care if a particular stock is not valued enough. The only factor that you have to take into account is the historical data of the stock and what information thisdata conveys about where the stock might be in the future.

There are three major assumptions that comprises the basis of TechnicalAnalysis:

1. The prices of stocks move according
to trends

2. History will repeat itself
The stock market will discount everything
Let's discuss each assumption in detail:

1. The Prices of Stocks Move According
to Trends

The movement of stock prices according to trends is a fundamental concept in technical analysis. When the market is experiencing a trend, the possible movement of price in the future is more likely to be in similar movement of the trend than to be opposite of it. Many trading strategies founded on technical analysis are based on this assumption.

2. History Will Repeat Itself

Another crucial concept in technical analysis is that history has the tendency to repeat itself, mostly in terms of the movement of price. The replicability nature of the movement of prices is heavily related to psychological behavior of traders. Players in the market tend to provide a constant response to similar market scenarios in a certain period of time. In technical analysis, traders use chart patterns to study the movements in the market and make sense of current trends. Even though most of these charts have been used for decades, these are still applicable because they show patterns in the movement of prices, which usually repeat over time.

This repetitive nature is applicable not only for stocks. It is also relevantto other instruments/markets such as forex, futures, commodities, and many more. In this guide, we often cite stocks in our example, but you should bear in mind that this replicability is applicable to any kind of asset. As a matter offact, technical analysis is often associated with forex and commodities, whereplayers are mostly day traders.

3. The Stock Market Will Discount Everything

A primary feedback about technical analysis is that it is only looking into the price movement, and it ignores the basic factors of the company. But an assumption of technical analysis points out that in any period, the price of a stock actually reflects everything that can have influence on the company, which includes the fundamental factors.

Day traders who are using technical analysis believe that the fundamental factors of the company, along with market psychology and economic factors, are all considered into the stock, which actually makes it unnecessary to look into these factors independently. Hence, the price movement is the onlyfactor that should be looked into. Remember, according to the technicaltheory the price movement is the product of the demand and supply for a certain stock.

Technical Analysis versus Fundamental Analysis

After understanding the philosophy behind technical analysis, the next step is to understand how it really works. One way to look closely into the nature of technical analysis is to place it against fundamental analysis.

Fundamental analysis and technical analysis are the two primary strategies in studying the stock market. As we have already mentioned above,technical analysis evaluates the movement of price of a certain stock and usesthis data to project the possible movements in the future.

On the other hand, fundamental analysis studies the economic indicators, which are known as fundamentals. We will discuss the specific of these two strategies - the main criticisms on technical analysis and how these two couldbe used to guide your decision in day trading.

The Differences between Technical Analysis and Fundamental Analysis

We can look into the differences between technical

analysis and fundamental analysis if we take a closer look on their charts/financial statements, time horizon, and trading/investing.

Financial Statements and Charts

Basically, technical analysis is driven by charts, while fundamental analysis is driven by financial statements. Through fundamental analysis, a trader can study the income statement, cash flow statement, and balance sheet to determine the value of the company. Financially, the trader can measure the intrinsic value of the company, which makes it actually easier to make a decision. If the stock priceis being traded below the intrinsic value, then there is high possibility that the investment is good. Even though this can be overly simplified, (fundamental analysis is more than just poring over financial statements and balance sheets), this basic concept is true.

Through technical analysis, the trader does not consider the intrinsic

value of the company, because of the assumption that these are all already integrated in the price of the stock. Day traders who are using technical analysis assume that all the information they need to make a decision are already manifested in the charts.

Time Horizon

More often than not, day traders who use fundamental analysis takes longer timeframe to analyze the market compared to day traders who are using technical analysis. While fundamental analysis usually looks into data in a span of years, technical analysis can be used for a time period of weeks, days, and even minutes. The varying timeframes that these two strategies use is caused by the nature of the investment style that they follow. It may take years for the valueof the company to reflect in the market. Hence, when a fundamental analyst projects the intrinsic value, the gain will not be secured until the market price of the stock increases to match this value. This kind of investing is known as value investing, and it is based on the assumption that the short-term marketis not true, and the price of a certain stock will rectify itself in due time. This "due time" could signify a timeframe of as long as several years, in certain instances.

Moreover, the numbers that a fundamentalist evaluates

are only issued over longer time frames. The company's financial statements are filed every quarter and the changes in the profits per share are not reflected on aneveryday basis such as price and volume data. You should also take note that the fundamentals are the actual nature of the business. Even though there is a new management team in the company, the changes will not be influential in the market overnight. It takes time to come up with new products, implement marketing campaigns, improve supply chains, and more.

Hence, a part of the reason that fundamental analysis uses a long-term approach is because the data they use to analyze a stock is produced much slower compared to the volume and price data crucial in technical analysis.

Investing / Trading

Aside from the timeframe approach, fundamental analysis and technical analysis are also different in terms of the goals of a sale (or a purchase) of a certain stock. Generally, technical analysis is ideal for trading, while fundamental analysis is ideal for investment. Stock investors purchase assets that they conclude could rise in value, while traders purchase asset that they conclude they could sell immediately at a higher price. The line between an investment and a trade could be blurry, but it can provide the distinction between the two stock concepts.

Criticisms against Technical Analysis

Some naysayers view technical analysis as a form of a forbidden tactic. Infact, some stock investors are questioning the validity of technical analysis asa true discipline. But as time goes by, technical analysis has seen support in the financial markets and has enjoyed mainstream credibility today. Even though most analysts in the financial markets are using fundamental analysis,many of them including large broker firms are now using technical analysis, too.

Much of the negative perception about technical analysis is rooted on the academic theories, particularly the EMH or the Efficient Market Hypothesis. EMH states that the price of the market is always the right price. Any trading data has been already considered in the current stock price and so, anyattempt to look for undervalued stocks is unnecessary.

Weak Form Efficiency

In this version of EMH, all the data about the past stock prices are alreadyfactored in the prevailing price. Based on this version of EMH, you can project future movements through technical analysis, because the historical data have been all considered for, and so, analyzing the price movements of aparticular stock will offer no insight for its future movements.

Semi-Strong Form Efficiency

In the second version of EMH, fundamental analysis is also considered asuseless in searching for potential investment opportunities.

Strong Form Efficiency

This version of EMH claims that all data in the financial markets are all accounted for in the price of the stock and neither fundamental nor technical analysis could provide traders or investors with any advantage. Most financial analysts follow the weak form, thus, from its perspective, if technical analysis is effective, market efficiency can be called into question.

Operating Protocol - Part 1

Indicators and charts are one of the most important components when we talk about technical analysis. In addition to experience, coldness, and psychology, a good analyst cannot disregard a thorough knowledge of the graphs. The latter can represent different information and may appear in different forms.

In technical analysis, the graphs deserve particular attention because they represent the price dynamics of a given financial instrument and in a given period.

In the technical analysis, the most commonly used type of graph is certainly the candlestick chart, better known under the name of a Japanese candlestick chart. Before moving on to a detailed description of the candlestick chart, however, I would like to say a few words about two other charts, less used than candlestick charts, but which may be useful as they can help you understand the Japanese candlestick chart.

The price chart is shown on a Cartesian plane where:
•on the abscissa axis (the horizontal axis) the time is reported,
•on the ordinate axis (the vertical axis) the price is reported.

Given this premise, we can still say that the graphs refer to different time periods whether they are fractions of minutes, hours and days, if not even weeks, months or even years indicating different sizes of opening or closing, of maximums and minimums.

On the axis of the abscissas, we find a space called histogram of the volume, which represents the quantity of instruments exchanged during the period under examination.

In graphic analysis in the specific and more generally in the technical analysis, various types of graph are used.

Wedge

This is a continuation figure and is very similar to the triangle for 2 reasons:

- For the form;
- For the time it takes to form. This differs from the triangle that we will see below because the shape that forms is characterized by a strongly bullish or bearish inclination opposite to that of the current trend.

This means that:

- this chart consists of two convergent trend lines and takes about one tothree months to develop;
- in an uptrend, a falling wedge or "a descending wedge" can been countered;
- while in a bearish tendency a rising wedge or "an ascending wedge" candevelop.

As with the pennant and flag figures, the wedge can be found in the middle of a movement, thus allowing to calculate minimum targets.

The dynamics of the volumes see a decrease in the course of the formation of the pattern and it should go to be reduced for all the period of formation of the figure. On the contrary, they increase significantly when the trend line is broken, which is a typical feature of the wedge.

Pennant

This figure is also quite common in chart analysis. This figure together with the figure of the flag, which we will see immediately after the flag appears after an almost vertical movement and represents a pause in the trend.

Its characteristic is that it is presented as a symmetrical triangle which, however, has a maximum extension of 3 weeks. Most often, in bearishactions, the refinement time of the figure is even lower and is equal to one or maximum two weeks. The pennant is halfway to the bullish or bearish movement, with the obvious implications in calculating the minimum targets for the movement's arrival.

It will, therefore, be obvious that the volume decreases during the formation of the figure and should be low throughout the period of formation of the pattern. On the contrary, instead, they increase significantly when the trendline breaks, which identifies the pennant. These are accompanied by a similar trend in the range within which prices move.

Pennants, most often coincide with a contraction phase, which does not necessarily have an opposite inclination with respect to the basic trend.
Both this figure and the next develop within a rather short time frame. The third figure that we examine as announced is the Rectangle.

Rectangle

The rectangle is the simplest among the figures proposed by the technical analysis.

It identifies a phase of price congestion. In Technical Analysis, with this term, we mean a graphic formation in correspondence with which prices oscillate within a narrow range of values. This process takes place when the market moves sideways.

The pattern represents a break zone of the current trend in which prices move sideways. This also gives rise to the name of trading range or congestion area, a figure that represents a period of consolidation of the current trend that is resolved in the direction of the trend that preceded it. This represents a fundamental figure, to correctly identify the continuation pattern if not also the observation of the volumes.

Also, for this bullish figure, the rebounds must be accompanied by high volumes, with the corrections characterized by decreasing volumes. In the opposite case, instead, in the bearish rectangle, are the corrections to have more accentuated volumes.

Many investors, take advantage of the oscillations, selling to the top ofthe figure and buying at the minimum. However, those who use this approachrisk not exploiting the breaking of the pattern.

The figure usually takes from one to three months to improve, and the minimum target is represented by the translation of the height of the rectanglewhen the price breaks the figure.
Prices move within a fixed band identified by a support and resistance.

The rectangles can also be configured as inversion figures, depending on the context in which they are formed. It is therefore evident how the congestion phases identify a moment in which the market expresses considerable uncertainty and awaits new information to decide the future trend. Unlike the contraction phases (in which the continuous reduction in volatility identifies in an increasingly precise manner the moment in which the market will receive the information that awaits) a figure of congestionlike the rectangle does not allow to identify sufficiently in advance the moment in which the breakout will take place.

The operational cues that this figure can provide are basically of two types:
The first requires waiting for the exit of prices from

the congestion zone initially identified. This exit must necessarily be classified as a breakout and therefore must be characterized by an increase in volumes and volatility.

- The second operational step derives from the possibility of exploiting the lateral movement of prices to buy close to the identified support and sellwhen the values are near the top of the figure again.

The fifth figure, object of study concerns the triangle.

Triangle

In technical analysis, the triangle is a consolidation figure and is used to verify the continuation of the main trend. This is a pattern that lasts a few months when there is a pause in the current trend with prices that oscillate in an increasingly narrow area.

The figure has the following characteristics:

- The triangle must have a minimum of four reaction points; two superiors, and two inferiors; the first ones necessary to trace the upper trend line, the seconds necessary to draw the lower trend line.

- A time limit for its resolution characterizes the triangle. Usually, the prices break the triangle at a point between two thirds and three quarters ofthe depth of the triangle.

- The volumes in the formation phase of the triangle waves, lose strength and then explode when the trend line that delimits the figure breaks.

- The minimum target for price trends is calculated by projecting themaximum height of the triangle.

The figure in question can present itself according to three differentstructures:

symmetrical triangle which has the trend lines that delimit itthat are convergent. Prices tend to move in a range that gradually becomes narrower with the passing of the sessions, due to a constant reduction of the maximums, and also due to a constant reduction of the minimums.

In this figure, there will be a greater conviction on the

part of the bearish and is often found during a downward trend. The reduction in the range within which prices move, occurs only thanks to an increase in the minimum, while the maximums remain almost unchanged. Justsuch behavior makes evident the greater pressure of the buyers withrespect to the sellers and attributes to this figure a bullish value.

The figure represents a symmetrical structure, which makes it difficult to interpret. In the third case, on the other hand, we speak of an ascending triangle, characterized by an upper line of flat demarcation and a line, the lower, ascending line. This patternindicates a greater strength of the uptrend and is often found duringan uptrend

Regardless of the configuration, whether symmetrical, ascending or descending, it is possible to calculate the target of the figure, i.e. the level thatprices should reach in the phase following the breakout.

This is calculated by projecting, from the breaking point, the "base" of thetriangle, i.e. the maximum

width that the figure recorded during its formation.
The sixth figure in question concerns the
formation of broadening.

Broadening

This represents a rather rare figure, classified as a variant of the triangle but which presents a contrary opening, with divergent trend lines. It is afigure that occurs at the end of a trend, usually bullish.

The dynamics of the volumes are different from that of the triangles, as the volume gradually expands together with the increase in price oscillation.
The seventh figure that we are going
to examine concerns the diamond.

Rounding and Spike

This represents one of the many figures of inversions, which presents itself as a slow and gradual movement on the lows that will first have a slight downward, then lateral and then shows a growing movement.

The pattern is one of the slowest of all the graphic

analysis and is usually identifiable on longer-term charts.

It is really difficult to establish the precise moment in which the figurecan be considered complete, if not after the first substantial rises. More difficult, it will be to identify upward targets.

Spike is also very special. The figures in question show, without any transition period, a sudden reversal of the quotations. An inversion accompanied by an explosion of volumes.

Due to its characteristics, the figure in question is difficult to identify in advance.

Operating Protocol- Part 2

Day trading strategies are important if you want to capitalize on regular, minor price fluctuations. A reliable, efficient approach depends on in-depth technological research, maps, metrics and trends to forecast potential market fluctuations. This page will provide you a detailed rundown of beginnertrading strategies, going all the way to intermediate, automatic, and even asset-specific strategies. It will also explain some of the geographical variations that you need to be mindful of, as well as guide you in the direction of some valuable tools. At the end of the day, though, you'll need to consider a trading approach that fits your unique trading style and specifications.

Always, make sure your choice of broker fits a day-to-day trading approach:

•Outstanding speed of trading execution,

•Price action data (+ Level 2 if possible)

•Willingness to sell directly from graphs,

•Trade automation,

•Stop losses and take profit orders

5 Day Trading Strategies

1. Breakout

Breakout techniques focus on when the price reaches the specified amount on the chart, with decreased volume. The breakout trader reaches a long role after the commodity or defense breaks through the resistance.Alternatively, you reach a short role as soon as the stock falls below the cover.

When an asset or commodity sale moves over the defined price limit, uncertainty typically increases, and stocks frequently shift in the direction ofa breakout.

You ought to find the right trade instrument. When doing so, keep inmind the level of support and resistance of the asset. The more frequently the price crosses these thresholds, the more justified and significant they are.

Entry Points

This part is really good and straightforward. Prices set to close and above the thresholds of resistance need a bearish role. Prices set to close and below the support point ought to be.

Plan your exits

Using the recent success of the commodity to set a fair price target. Usingchart patterns makes this method much more precise. You can measure the average recent price changes to set a target. If the average market swing has been 3 points in the past five price swings that would be a realistic target. When you have achieved that target, you will leave the trade and make an earn.

2. Scalping

Scalping is one of the most common techniques. It's especially commonin the forex market, and looks to capitalize on minute price shifts. Thedriving force here is quantity. You're going to look to sell as long as the exchange is competitive. It's a fast-paced and thrilling way to deal, but it can be dangerous.

3. Momentum

Popular in beginners trading strategies, this approach focuses on acting on news outlets and recognizing important developments with high-volume help.There's still at least one stock that travels about 20-30% a day, and there's plenty of potential. You just hang on to your spot until you see signs of turnaround and then get out of it.

Alternatively, the price drop will fade. This way round the demand target is as soon as the amount starts to decline.

This technique is quick and effective when used correctly. Nonetheless, you need to make sure that you are aware of future news and results reports. Just a few seconds on each exchange will make all the difference to the earnings at the end of the day.

4. Reversal

While intensely contested and highly harmful as used by beginners, reverse trading is used all over the planet. It's also known as pattern investing,pull back trending, and mean reversal strategy.

This approach tests the simple logic when you seek to compete againstthe pattern. You need to be able to define potential pitfalls reliably, plus forecast their power. You require in-depth business awareness and expertise to do so successfully.

The 'daily change' technique is known to be a special case of reversal trading, because it relies on purchasing and selling low and high pullbacks/reverses on a daily basis.

5. Using Pivot Points

A day trading turning point technique can be brilliant for detecting and operating on a crucial level of support and/or resistance. This is especially useful in the forex industry. In addition, range-bound traders can be used to define entry points, while pattern and breakout traders can use trigger points to spot key thresholds that need to be reached for a move to count as a breakout.

Calculating Pivot Points

The pivot point is known as the rotation point. You use the high and low prices of the previous day, plus the security closing price, to determine the pivot point.

Notice that if you determine a focal point using price information over a fairly limited timeframe, precision is always diminished.

Here's how to calculate a pivot point?

Central Pivot Point (P) = (High + Low + Close)/3

You can measure the support and resistance

rate using the pivot point.

You would need to use the following

formulas to do this:

•First Resistance (R1) = (2*P) – Low

•First Support (S1) = (2*P) – High

Limit Your Losses

It is especially important if you use the margin. Requirements that are normally large for day traders. When you sell moderately, you become highly vulnerable to sudden price swings. Sure, this means the opportunity forgreater profit, but it also implies the risk of significant losses. Luckily, you can make stop-losses.

Stop-loss monitors the risk to you. In a short position, you can put a stop- loss above a recent high; you can place it below a recent low for long positions. You can make it based on uncertainty, too.

For example, the stock price falls by $ 0.05 per minute, and you put a stop-loss $ 0.15 away from your order of entry.

One of the common methods is to set up two stop-losses. First, you place a physical stop-loss order at a particular price point. That is going to be the only money you can afford to waste. Second, you're generating an emotional stop-loss. Place this at the stage where the submission requirements havebeen broken. So, if the trade is going to make an unanticipated switch, you'll make a quick escape.

Forex Trading Strategies

Forex plans are dangerous by nature, because you intend to maximize your gains over a brief amount of time.

Cryptocurrency Trading Strategies

The thrilling and volatile cryptocurrency market provides plenty of options for day traders to turn. Simply using simple tactics to make the most of this competitive market.

Stock Trading Strategies

Day trading strategies for stocks are based on many of the same ideas, and all of the techniques mentioned above can be used.

Spread Betting Strategies

Spread betting helps you to gamble on a large range of financial stocks without necessarily buying the asset. Plus, the techniques are fairly basic.

CFD Strategies

Designing a successful day-to-day trading approach can be difficult. However, go for an instrument such as a CFD and the task could be a little simpler.

CFDs are concerned with the disparity between the

entrance and departure of the exchange. Recent years have seen an increase in success. It isso you will make a profit as the underlying asset changes in addition to the position held, without actually having to buy the underlying asset.

Regional Differences

Global markets come with different challenges and obstacles to conquer. Day trading techniques for the Indian market cannot be as successful when implemented in Australia. For example, certain countries may be distrustful of the press, and the economy does not respond in the same way that you would expect them to come home.

Regulations are another element to be weighed. Indian approaches can be customized to suit particular rules, such as large minimum equity reserves in margin accounts. Yeah, go online and find out ambiguous laws won't have aneffect on your plan until you put your hard-earned money on the table.

You can also note that various nations have different tax gaps to leap through. When you are headquartered in the West but want to apply your usual day trading tactics in the Philippines, you need to do your homework first.

What kind of tax do you have to pay for?

Are you going to have to spend for overseas

and/or domestically? Small tax dissimilarities

may have a big effect on the day-to-day earnings.

Risk Management

Stop-loss

If you don't handle the chance, you lose more than
you can afford and getout of the game before you know
it. That's why you can still use a stop-loss.

The price may seem to be moving in the
direction you wanted, but itcould be reversed at any
moment. Stop-loss regulates the chance. You're going
to leave the exchange and then take a marginal loss if
the commodityor defense doesn't come in.

Savvy traders typically do not gamble more than 1%
of their balance of accounts in a single trade. And if you
have $ 27,500 in your portfolio, you could lose up to $
275 a deal.

Position size

This will also help you to select the correct size of
the role. The value of the position is the number of

shares taken in a single exchange. Take the difference between the entry fee and the stop-loss price. For example, if your entry point is $ 12 and your stop loss is $ 11.80, then your cost is $ 0.20 per share. Now, to find out how many deals you can make in a single deal, divide $ 275 by $ 0.20. You can take up to 1,375 shares in a position. It is thehighest place you should take to adhere to the 1% danger limit.

Often, verify if there is adequate space in the stock/asset to accommodate the scale of the position you are using. In addition, bear in mind that if you take a position that is too large for the market, you may experience slippage on your entry and stop-loss.

Practice 4:

Based on previous Practical, write down entry and exit point on selected market/stock, selected instrument, following selected strategy. Start to track the record of your trade, before investing real money, it will be helpful, at thebeginning.

Scalping

Traders can be divided into three types: swing traders, day traders, and scalpers. The three methods can be mixed up together, which is my preferred mode of operation.

Scalping refers to very short-term trades. Swing traders hold stocks over to the next day, and day traders generally try to get as much from the stock aspossible within one day of trading. Both swing and day traders generally basetheir systems on technical analysis with a touch of fundamental analysis.

Scalpers are based a hundred percent on technical analysis. Their goal is the very short term. Changes of just a few cents for several seconds up to some minutes are enough. This means that in order to earn a livelihood from the market, scalpers need to trade in relatively larger amounts than day or swing traders. Scalpers with little backing (which is, sadly, the case for most of them) make up for what their pocket lacks by trading in financial products which can be leveraged more than the typical leverage of the world of stock trading. These may include futures, leveraged twenty times more, options,and of course FOREX (foreign exchange) which can reach leveraging of upto 500 times more, expressed as 500:1 margin. The absurdity is that trading inthese strongly-leveraged products is harder and incredibly riskier than stock trading. Nonetheless, the dream of "striking it rich quick" draws people with no funds and no experience into the hardest areas of trading, where they will often begin, and almost invariably end, their trading careers.

Scalping techniques

The first condition: you need to keep your finger on the mouse, and your eyes glued to the screen. You need to give your full attention to the stock. You must buy and sell with precise LIMIT orders. You must absolutely NOTchase the stock, because with scalping, profit or loss is measured in just a fewcents. In many cases, I place an exit order in advance. For example: if I buy 3000 shares at $20 and anticipate an increase of 30 cents, I will set a sell limitorder in my trading platform of:

- 1000 shares at 20.15
- 1000 shares at 20.25

- And wait with my finger on the mouse for the first sign of weakness in order to sell the remaining 1000 shares

SMART MONEY Scalps are meant to be short term, and are thereforenot executed in small quantities. Trading in small quantities of shares causes the "small-money syndrome" and leads to failure.

Scalping is not executed in small quantities of shares. New traders scalping in small quantities, such as 300 shares, find themselves caught in the trap of negligible profits, or as the phenomenon is known, the "small-money syndrome." Selling 100 shares for a profit of 15 cents seems like too small a yield, so they will try to drag the trade out for a few more cents, and usually discover that they have waited too long before selling. The stock pulls back down by 10 cents, so it does not pay to sell because the profit is even less now, and they wait a bit longer. Then the stock returns to their entry point, or even below it, and the scalping ends in a loss!

With large quantities of shares, by contrast, a decent profit is earned with each partial trade locked in, without the need to cope with the small-money syndrome.

The One Cent Scalp

Cent scalping is a trading method geared at making profits of one or just afew cents, from light intraday fluctuations in stocks with "locked prices." Stocks with locked prices are stocks in which hundreds if not thousands of traders are operating, executing bids and asks at one cent above or below the stock's traded price. This is not a classic trading method based on noticeable intraday fluctuations resulting from breakouts, breakdowns, or direction changes. In contrast with everything we have learned so far, scalping for one cent is based chiefly on lack of volatility. I wish to emphasize that this is not my area of specialization, or even a method.

One Cent Scalping and the
Commission Barrier

The first condition for participating in this method is to have a large trading account. If you want to profit from the movement of one cent and stillovercome the barrier of commission, you need to operate with no less than 10,000 shares. A profit of one cent on 10,000 shares is worth $100, from which commission must still be deducted. The commissions with this methodare the key to success or failure.

Here is an example: let us say that you profited one cent on 10,000 shares, producing $100. Let's assume that you pay a commission of one cent per share, and you bought 10,000 shares. That totals $100 profit, cancelledout by the commission, and when you sell, that costs another $100. Altogether, a loss of $100. Even if you paid commission of one- tenth of a cent, totaling $20 for both buy and sell executions, you have still left 20% of your profit with the broker.

This may sound reasonable to you, but you must also take into accountthe sad fact that when you lose (at least 30% of your executions will end upas losses), the loss plus the commission will total $120. The weighted average is definitely to your detriment.

The solution: unlike the method of charging one cent per share, whichwill only be worthwhile if you operate in quantities of up to 2000 shares per click, when you trade in large fixed amounts, you need to ask your broker to define a different commission system based on the Per Trade Commission Plan rather than the Per Share Commission Plan. If you trade in large amounts, it is probable that you will be able to close on a price of $3 to $6 perclick of the button, unlimited in quantity.

In actuality, large-scale traders usually receive commissions rather than pay them. How? When you set your bid and ask orders and wait for their execution, you are adding liquidity to the market! When you do that, as we have already learned, you receive a commission of $2 per 1000 shares from the ECN. With a simple calculation, you can understand that the relatively small quantity of 10,000 shares will bring you an ECN return of 0.2 cents per share, which is $20, while you paid only $6. What would happen with a quantity of 100,000 shares? The ECN return is worth $200, while the commission you pay is still $6. Can you see where this is going? I amfamiliar with traders who make their living from buying and selling a share atexactly the same price, for profits of hundreds of dollars from the ECN returnalone. If they're lucky, they also manage to earn another cent per share.

One Cent Scalping: The Method First find a low-priced stock

This should ideally be in the $5 to $10 range, with low volatility and a volume of tens of millions of shares per day.

The candidates change during different periods of market activity, volatility, and price. Remember that volatility is this method's worst enemy. Just imagine how much you could lose if the stock moved ten cents against you! This is also why you MUST operate according to the following rules:

1. The stock must be moving sideways with no trend, or in industryterms, the stock must have a locked price
2. The stock must show no volatility and movement of up to 5-10 cents per day
3. The market is moving sideways with no trend (generally occurs duringlunch hours)
4. The stock is priced up to $10.
5. You can buy cheap stocks in large quantities even if your name is not Warren Buffet

6. The stock shows large trading volume of tens of millions per day

The simplest way to choose a stock is to fish it out of the list that always contains the "top ten" high volume stocks traded on NASDAQ or NYSE. Notice that I do not relate to stocks that made it into the list by chance, but those which are on that listing constantly. On some days, you might choose Bank of America (BAC) or Intel (INTC), Microsoft (MSFT) or others. Citigroup (C) used to be the scalpers' favorite as long as its price hovered around the $4 mark in volumes of hundreds of millions of shares per day, before the reverse split was executed, as already described.

When you bring these stocks up on your screen, you will see intraday volumes of tens if not hundreds of millions of shares, and enormous numbers of bidders and askers. Many of them are playing the one cent game.

Who in fact shifts the stock if no one wants it to move more than one cent? Of course, this would not be the scalpers working at the single cent level, because they are basically locking the price and preventing movement. The real change comes from the public and from funds bidding and asking with long-term investment in mind, and they are not interested in whether thestock has gone up or down one cent.

Let's assume you have chosen your stock and it's time to trade. The operation itself is fairly simple but requires a good deal of experience. First, even if the price is moving sideways, examine the overall market trend and the stock's trend. If the trend is up, you will want to execute a long ratherthan a short, and vice versa. Now you need to enter your buy limit order in the BID, and wait patiently until sellers hit your bid. The moment you have bought the desired quantity, you enter a sell limit order on the ASK side, witha profit target of 1 to 3 cents, and wait for buyers to hit your ask in thereverse direction.

Notice that there is no need to use the short order, since for most of the trading platforms the regular SELL will operate exactly like a short. Now thatyou have sold the quantity you bought at a profit, and added to that sale a double quantity, you are in a short and therefore need to position a double quantity on the BID side with a targeted profit of 1 to 3 cents, repeating the cycle. Once the market becomes more volatile, and based on the premise that you are on the right side of market direction, you need to cancel the exit orderand try to profit from a few more cents beyond the original profit target.

Here some useful websites for monitoring stocks and markets :Trading View Screener, Finviz, Trade Ideas, Motley Fool.

Trading Platforms

A trading platform is software used for trading managing market positions through a fiscal intermediary such as an internet broker. Online trading programs are often provided by agents either at no cost or at adiscount fee in exchange for keeping a funded account or making a predetermined variety of transactions each month. The finest trading platforms provide a mixture of powerful features and reduced prices.

Principles of Trading Platform

A trading platform is the application that allows traders and investors to place transactions and track accounts through fiscal intermediaries. Oftentimes, trading programs will come bundled together with different characteristics, such as real time quotations, charting programs, news feeds, as well as superior research. Platforms might also be especially tailored to certain markets, like stocks, monies, alternatives, or futures markets.

They're characterized by ease-of-use along with also

a range of useful features, such as news feeds and graphs, for investor education and study. Prop platforms, on the other hand, are customized platforms developed with big brokerages to match their particular needs and trading style.

Dealers use an assortment of different trading platforms based on their trading design and quantity.

Selecting a Platform

When picking between trading platforms, both investors and traders should consider both the charges involved and attributes available. Day dealers along with other short-term traders might need attributes like grade two quotations and market manufacturer depth charts to help out with decision-making, whilst choices traders might need tools which are particularly designed to picture options plans.

Fees are another significant consideration when picking trading platforms. By way of instance, traders that use scalping for a trading approach may gravitate towards platforms using reduced prices. Generally, lower prices are almost always preferable but there might be trade-offs totake into account but low prices might not be valuable if they interpret to fewer attributes and informational study.

Some trading platforms can be reverted to a particular intermediary or even agent, though other trading platforms are only accessible when working with a specific broker or agent. Because of this, investors should also consider the standing of the intermediary or agent before committing to a certain trading platform to implement trades and handle their account.

Ultimately, trading platforms might have particular requirements to be eligible due to their usage. By way of instance, day trading platforms might require that dealers have $25,000 at equity inside their account and be qualified for margin trading, whereas alternatives platforms might require approval to exchange a variety of kinds of choices prior to having the ability to utilize the trading platform.

Popular Trading Platforms

There are hundreds--or even thousands--of different trading platforms, including those four popular choices:

• Interactive Agents: Interactive Brokers is the most popular trading platform for professionals using reduced fees and accessibility to markets across the world.

• Trade Station: Trade Station is a favorite trading platform for algorithmic dealers who prefer to perform trading strategies utilizing automated scripts developed with Easy Language.

• Robinhood: Robinhood is a commission-free trading platform aimed at millennial. It started off as a portable program and today has a web interface too. The platform makes cash from many sources, from interest on money in its account to promoting order flow to big brokerages.

• The very popular platform for all foreign exchange (forex) Marketplace participants is Metaorder that will be a trading platform that interfaces with several distinct brokers. Its MQL scripting language is now a favorite tool for those seeking to automate trading in monies.

Selecting the Proper Day-Trading Software

Computer software have made it simple to automate trading, particularly for short term intensive tasks like day trading, making the use of trading program popular. The discussion continues within the profit potential which will be realistically derived from day-trading actions utilizing online trading platforms, as broker fees and commissions are believed to eliminate the significant part of available gain possible. It thus becomes extremely important to choose the ideal day-trading software using a cost-benefit analysis, evaluation of its applicability to individual trading requirements and strategies, in addition to the features and functions you want.

Day trading is a currency trading action at which purchase or market positions are accepted and closed on precisely the exact same trading daywith a goal to earn gains in smaller price differentials on large purchase volumes by regular buying and selling, typically on leverage.

What's Day-Trading Software?

Day-trading software comprises a computer program, generally supplied by brokerage companies, to assist customers execute their day-trading actionsin an efficient and timely way. They frequently automate analysis and input transactions in their own that allow traders to reap gains that would be tough to attain by mere mortals. By way of instance, a day dealer might find it impossible to manually monitor two technical indicators (such as 50- and 200-day moving averages) on three distinct shares of her or his choice, but an automatic day-trading software can certainly take action and put trades after the set standards are satisfied.

The characteristics and functions available can vary from 1 softwarepackage to another and can arrive in various versions. Aside from agents, independent sellers also give day-trading applications, which often have moreadvanced capabilities.

An example: Assume stock ABC is dual-listed on either the New York Stock Exchange (NYSE) and on Nasdaq. You're searching for arbitrage chances and there's a day-trading software available to this. You prepare the following:

Select inventory ABC for arbitrage and choose two markets (NYSE and Nasdaq) for trading.

Assuming both thighs of intraday exchange prices you a total of $0.10 per share for commission and brokerage; you plan to search for cost differentials between the two markets in excess of that sum. So that you place (state $0.20 or over) as the cost differential--

i.e., the program must execute a simultaneous purchase and sell purchase just when the bidding and ask prices on the 2 markets are different by $0.20 (or much more).

Establish the amount of stocks to be purchased and sold in 1 sequence (say 10,000 stocks).
Permit this installment go live.

Say the Program explains that ABC has estimates of $62.10 on NYSE and $62.35 on Nasdaq (a differential of $0.25) for orders of over the established limit of 10,000 shares. The day-trading applications will commence trade as it fulfills with the specified standards, and will sendorders into the two trades (purchase at reduced priced and market at even higher priced). If everything goes well, this day-trading application will create ((62.35 -- 62.10) -- 0.10 = 0.15) * (10,000) = $1,500 of net gain for your dealer super-fast.

Further improvements in the aforementioned applications may include stop-loss attributes, state if just your purchase trade gets implemented but not the market. How should the day-trading applications proceed using the long standing? A few options can be contained as improved features in the program:

- Proceed to search for market chances

at identified costs for a particular moment. If no opportunities are recognized in the designated period, square off the place at reduction.

• Change into an averaging strategy, purchase more shares at lower coststo decrease the overall cost

Features and Functionality

What described above is an example of arbitrage where gambling chancesare short-lived. A good deal of these kinds of day-trading actions can be installed via day-trading applications and so it's extremely important to pick the perfect one fitting your requirements. Some features of great day-trading applications:

• Platform freedom: unless a dealer is operating exceptionally intricate calculations for Day-trading requiring high-end computers that are dedicated, it makes sense to use an online program offering. Benefits include connectivity from anyplace, no manual installments of updates and no maintenance prices. But if you're using highly sophisticated algorithms which need sophisticated computing, then it's far better to consider committed computer-based installable applications, even though that will be pricey.

• Your particular needs daily trading: are you currently observing a straightforward day-trading approach of moving-average monitoring on Stocks, or are you seeking to implement an intricate delta-neutral trading strategy including stocks and options? Do you require a currency feed or are you currently trading on specific products such as binary choices? Trusting the promises on stockbrokers' site content isn't enough to know that the offering. Request a trial version also completely evaluate it during the first phase. Alternately, check the screen-by-screen tutorial (if available) in the stockbroker or seller to clearly know the ideal match for the day-trading needs.

•Added Attributes: day trading efforts to capitalize on short-term price movements over the course of the day. Such short-term price movements are subsequently driven primarily by information and distribution and need (among other variables). Does your day-trading strategy demand information, graphs, grade two info, exclusive connectivity into specific markets (such as

OTC), special data feeds, etc.? If so, are those contained in the applications orwould the dealer need to subscribe to them individually from different resources, hence raising the price?

•Analytical Features: pay attention to this record of analytical features it provides.

•Technical.indicators/Pattern Recognition: for dealers who try to gain from calling the upcoming cost level and management, a wealth of technical indicators can be obtained. When the dealer finalizes the specialized indicators to follow along, they ought to guarantee that the day-trading program affirms the essential automation for efficient processing of transactions based on the desirable technical index.

Day trader Checklist, compile every day, before starting the trading day.

1. Have you rest?
2 Do you feel focused responsive?
3. Have you decided which markets/stocks to trade?

4. Have you selected which instruments to trade in any markets you wantto trade?

5. Have you selected the strategy for any markets you want to trade?Have you settled your daily maximum loss?

6. Have you settled your single trade maximum loss?

7. Has the market been subjected to abnormal volatility these days?

8. Has the market been subjected to abnormal price action that could also impact the instruments you want to trade?

There is today any relevant event that could abruptly impact market price action at some time? If Yes, have you planned to stop trading beforethat time?

Advices toBeginners on Day Trading

You have to understand that the stock market is a very volatile place, and anything can happen within a matter of a few seconds. You have to be prepared for anything that it throws at you. In order to prepare for it, youhave to make use of risk capital. Risk capital refers to money that you are willing to risk. You have to convince yourself that even if you lose the moneythat you have invested, then it will not be a big deal for you.

For that, you have to make use of your own money and not borrow from anyone, as you will start feeling guilty about investing it. Decide on a set number and invest it.

Research

You have to conduct thorough research on the market before investing in it. Don't think you will learn as you go. That is only possible if you at least know the basics. You have to remain interested in gathering information that is crucial for your investments, and it will only come about if you put in some hard work towards it. Nobody is asking you to stay up and go through thick textbooks. All you have to do is go through books and websites and gather enough information to help you get started on the right foot.

Stop loss

You have to understand the importance of a stop loss mechanism. A stop loss technique is used to safeguard an investment. Now say, for example, you invest $100 and buy shares priced at $5 each. You have to place a stop loss ataround $4 in order to stop it from going down any further. Now you will wonder as to why you have to place the stop loss and undergo one, well, by doing so, you will actually be saving your money to a large extent.

Take a loss

It is fine to take a loss from time to time. Don't think of it as a big hurdle. You will have the chance to convert the loss into a profit. You have to remainconfident and invested.

You can take a loss on a bad investment that was anyway not going your way. You can also take a loss on an investment that you think is a long hold and will not work for you in the short term. Taking a few losses is the onlyway in which you can learn to trade well in the market.

These form the different "do" of the stock market that will help you withyour intraday trades.

Below the "don't" of day trading

No planning

Do not make the mistake of going about investing in the market without aplan in tow. You have to plan out the different things that you will do in the market and go about it the right way. This plan should include how much youwill invest in the market, where you will invest, how you will go about it etc. No planning will translate to getting lost in the stock market, which is not a good sign for any investor.

Over rely on a broker

You must never over-rely on a broker. You have to make your own decisions and know what to do and when.

The broker will not know whether an investment is

good for you. He will only be bothered about his profits. If he is suggesting something, then you should do your own research before investing in the stock. The same extends to emails that you might receive through certain sources. These emails are spams and meant to dupe you. So, don't make the mistake of trusting everything that you read.

Message boards

You have to not care about message boards. These will be available onthe Internet and are mostly meant to help people gather information. Butthere will be pumpers and bashers present there. Pumpers will force people tobuy a stock just to increase its value, and bashers will force people to sell all their stocks just because they want the value to go down. Both these types arerisky, as they will abandon the investors just as soon as their motive is fulfilled. So, you have to be quite careful with it.

Calculate wrong

Some people make the mistake of calculating wrong. They will not be adept at math and will end up with wrong figures. This is a potential dangerto all those looking to increase their wealth potential.

If you are not a good at calculating, then download an app that will do it for you or carry a calculator around to do the correct calculations. The reasonis to make the right calculations and increase your wealth potential.

Copy strategies

Do not make the mistake of copying someone else's strategies. You have to come up with something that is your own and not borrowed from someone else. If you end up borrowing, then you will not be able to attain the desired results. You have to sit with your broker and come up with a custom strategy that you can employ and win big.

These form the different "don't" of the stock market that will help you keep troubles at bay.

The main tools used in Day Trading

Just like starting any other business or profession, you need a few important tools to begin day trading. Basically, you need a broker and a platform to execute your orders. These are the tools that you will certainly need to function as a day trader.

As explained, you also need a stock scanner to help

you find a watch list and look for potential setups in real-time. On top of a stock scanner, it is idealto be part of a trading community.

Day Trading Broker

You need a reliable broker for day trading. You don't need a popular broker; you need a reliable one. Remember, your broker is your vehicle to trade. Even if you are trading properly, you can lose money if you have a badbroker.

There are numerous brokers out there with different software and price schemes. Some are cheap but terrible, and some offer super service butexpensive. The following are the top brokers used by day traders around the world:

- E*TRADE
- TD Ameritrade
- Trade station
- Interactive Brokers
- Fidelity

But one of the main concerns for day traders is commission, or how muchis the broker going to take with every trade you make.

Most brokers will earn from your trades whether you win or lose thetrade. Therefore, savvy day traders are looking to save on trading costs as much as possible.

However, the trading cost should not be your only concern. You should also balance this factor with other features of the broker that can help you become more successful, like the tools you can use, research capacity, and trading platform.

So, while the trading cost is an essential factor, it is not the only concern you need to consider.

You must also check with the current rules for day trading in your region.For example, in the United States, day traders should maintain at least
$25,000 of equity in their accounts before they can trade as stipulated by the rules of the Financial Industry Regulatory Authority (FINRA).

Market Data and Trading Platform

You can be successful in your trades if you know how to execute your trades in a jiffy. You must be able to move in and out of the trades easily.

It can be a challenge to perform trades fast enough if your broker doesn't use a platform or software with hotkeys.

You need to make fast decisions so you can make extra dollars when the stock suddenly spikes. If the stock rises, you need to be able to place money in your account and make money from it fast. You certainly don't want to be bumbling with your orders. You need fast executions, which is why youreally need to use a good broker as well as a platform for quick order execution.

Stocks Scanner and Watch List

One of the common concerns among new traders does not know thestocks to trade. Every day, thousands of stocks move in the market. However, looking for a setup that is an excellent fit for your risk tolerance and consistent with your day trading strategy can be difficult.

You need to use a scanner to browse the market and look for good trades.The most popular stock scanners for day traders are the following:

- Stock Rover

- Cartmill

- Finviz

- Stock Fetcher

- Community of Traders

Even though day trading can be really exciting, it is also quite tricky andcan be emotionally overwhelming.

It is best to join a community of retail traders and ask them questions. Consult them whenever necessary, learn new strategies, and receive some expert insights and alerts about the stock market. But don't forget that you also need to contribute to the community.

You can also talk to each other and share screens and platforms so youcan watch each other as you trade. It can be a fun, interactive environment, and you can learn from each other. Through this, you can gain more knowledge and experience in day trading.

You will meet experienced traders in an online community whom you canlearn much from, and you can also help other newbie traders in exploring this lucrative business.

If you join an online community, you will see that other day traders lose money often. It can make you feel good to see that losing trades is quite common in this area, and everyone, including seasoned traders, still loses money in the process.

Bear in mind that you need to be an independent thinker. Basically, people may change when they join groups. They become more impulsive andunquestioning, nervously looking for a leader whose trades they can mimic. They respond with the crowd rather than using their own minds.

Members of the online community may be influenced by some trends, butthey could lose a lot of money if the trends suddenly reverse. Don't forgetthat successful traders are usually independent thinkers.

You must develop good judgment so you can decide when to trade and when not to trade.

Building a Trading Plan

Two trading plans are never the same because no traders are exactly alike. You'll be developing your unique plan based on experience, and could be making subtle or even large changes for a period of time. The plan will consider your experience, risk tolerance, your willingness to be honest with yourself – and how well you learn to adapt to survive. Here a list of things you may want to consider:

1. Skill Level, Experience, and Practice

Are you ready to trade? Have you tested your use of candlesticks, the MACD, and have you practiced enough to sense some rhythm in the market's movements? Trading is a battle of give and take, so prepare for that. As you practice prior to using real-money, you will improve very rapidly at first. Keeping a good trading log is essential, sometimes you find easy adjustmentsto make, and you identify areas that you need to give more thought and experience. If you are new to trading online, you will enjoy learning to use the software, reading the charts, and practice your ideas on trading in realtime with live quotes. The learning curve can be like a video game. At first you are getting the lay of the land and learning how all the controls work. Soon, you get better and better and things you struggled with at first, start becoming second nature. When you start feeling ready to trade, put your practice trades in the trading log. Jot down things to look up later, or questions about your software, or the use of candlesticks and the MACD. I recommend you choose the NASDAQ100 Micro. The DJIA is only 50 centsa point but it is a very narrow index and news on one stock can really pushthe market unexpectedly. I also like the S&P500 Micro but the dollar value moves 2.5 times faster than the NASDAQ100; they are $5 and $2 respective per point. Using the NASDAQ100 has two advantages (in my opinion) over learning with the S&P500 Micro; the dollar fluctuation amount is smaller and the NASDAQ100 is not primarily driven by financial stocks. Of course, you can try any of the four you like; I just think that learning with one of them at first, is less confusing – and $2 a point is less risky than $5.

2. Determine and Set Your Risk Level

You might, for example, decide not to risk more than 1% to 5% of your account balance in a single day. If you lose that amount during a day, it is probably better to stop trading and wait to try another day. Trading while emotional can skew your training and judgement.

3. Set Goals and Risk-Reward Parameters

Give some serious thought to what risk/reward ratio you will set. For example, you might decide that you won't take a trade unless you feel the reward is at least 3 times the risk (3:1 ratio.) A lot of texts urge beginners to set weekly, monthly, and annual goal right away. Personally, I think it'smuch better to know more about the trading you are doing and to get some experience before you rush to put those demands on yourself. Goals are great but you have to get some experience before you realize what might berealistic.

4. Pre-Trade Homework

Before you begin trading, check what is going on around the world. Find out what economic reports and events and their posting times. There are a lot of free services that will either post and/or email you a proper list of the events of the day- usually early in the morning. These can include meetings, news events, FED meetings, wars/military actions, trade agreements, and economic reports.

5. Rules for Exit

The very hardest thing for almost all traders is learning to exit a tradewith a loss. You must learn to take losses before they become big losses. Not learning to be able to take a loss is the #1 reason traders go out-of-business. Write down your exit point to prevent a large loss - when you make a trade. You may not realize it, but professional traders lose more trades than they win.

When you do make a profit target, protect it. Don't give it back to the market. After you have learned the basics and due to practice gain some confidence, you will advance to trading multiple numbers of contracts at once. Multiple contracts do offer some money-management advantages. For example, if you are trading two contracts and you hit your profit target point, you can take profits on one of those contracts, and keep the other going. Trading two contracts is a choice you can use - when putting in a trailing stoporder would be too close.

6. Setting Trade Entry Rules

Even though the exit rules are more important, you should start to form your trade entry rules. Here are some examples of how you can form your own rules:

In a DOWN trend day, I will not try to trade the UP intraday turns. (This would be going against the strongest trend of the day; this means more risk.) Conversely, in an UP-trend day, I will
not trade intraday down turns.

1. If you have missed a sudden and quick market move, you probably should not rush to make a new trade without thinking it through. Often during a day, a sudden and unexpected move happens; these often get overdone, and you can get trapped in the "bounce." (aka: whiplash)

2. Don't push a trade just because you get bored or impatient.

3. I might wait until resistance /support points, candlesticks, and MACD all concur before placing a trade - and I'll know my exit limit before I place atrade.

Find an entry point for a trade is the most difficult part of trading. What works perfectly one day, might not work at all the next. Computers very often will trade better than humans; in fact, almost 50% of NYSE stock trades are made by computers using algorithms – and still they lose on more than half the trades. One of the financial channels recently described a computer-trading algorithm that triggers on preselected words in Tweets and news headlines during the trading day.

The psychologically most difficult part of trading is the day when you have three losing trades in a row. This will often make you question the efficacy of your trading methods and destroy your confidence. Usually, the worst reaction you can have is to forget all your experience and rules, and start to trade randomly (without rules.) This is a very common reaction, and it seldom has positive results. Remember, your first responsibility is to protect your assets. Substituting hope during frustration can seriously damage your account balance. Some days, you will find the market just isn't working for you in spite of your best efforts. Better to stop, and come back the next day before your losses mount. I never met a trader that did NOT have days like this; the traders that last learn to deal with this. You won't be able to avoid experiencing this feeling. No amount of switching indicators, switching markets, or finding new strategies and methods, can ever insulate you from these days. Don't let one of these bad days force you into random trading or mounting losses. Remember hope is not a strategy. Your success will be found going through these days, not in going around them (which is futile.) These types of days are a part of trading whether you recognize them or not. I am reminded of the words of the late David Foster Wallace:

"Don't make your system too complicated because you will be making quick decisions. If you have ten or twenty conditions that must be met, you will find it difficult and nearly impossible to make trades."

The Best Strategies and Techniques to Start with Day Trading Strategies

Day trading strategies are basic when you are hoping to profit by visit, little value developments. A steady, compelling strategy depends on top to bottom technical examination, using graphs, indicators, and examples to foresee future value developments. This page will offer you a careful reprievedown of beginner trading strategies, working as far as possible up to cutting edge, computerized, and even resource explicit strategies.

It will likewise layout some local contrasts to know about, just as pointingyou toward some valuable assets. At last, however, you'll have to discover a day trading strategy that suits your particular trading style and prerequisites.

Likewise, guarantee your decision of intermediary suits strategy-based day trading. You will need things like;

• Excellent exchange execution speed,

• Price activity information (+ Level 2 if conceivable)

• Ability to exchange direct from diagrams,

- Trade robotization,

- Stop misfortunes and take benefit orders

- Etc. and so forth.

Trading Strategies for Beginners

Before you get hindered in an unpredictable universe of exceptionally technical indicators, center around the nuts and bolts of a basic day trading strategy. Many wrongly think you need an exceptionally muddled strategy to succeed intraday, yet frequently the clearer, the more powerful.

The Basics

Consolidate the priceless components underneath your strategy.

- Money management – Before you start, plunk down. Remember, best traders won't put over 2% of their capital at risk per exchange. You need toset yourself up for certain misfortunes on the off chance that you need to associate with when the successes begin coming in.

- Time management – Don't hope to make a fortune in the event that you just assign an hour or two every day to trading. You have to screen the markets and be vigilant for exchange openings continually.

- Education – Understanding market complexities isn't sufficient, and you additionally need to remain educated. Ensure you keep awake to date with market news and any occasions that will affect your advantage, for example,a move in a financial arrangement.

- Consistency –You have to let calculation, rationale, and your strategy direct you, not nerves, dread, or insatiability.

- Timing – The market will be unstable when it opens every day, and keeping in mind that accomplished day traders might have the option to peruse the examples and benefit, you ought to await your opportunity. So, keep down for the first 15 minutes, you've despite everything advanced hoursbeyond.

- Demo Account – An unquestionable requirement has device for any novice yet, in addition, the best spot to back test or explore different avenues regarding new, or refined, strategies for cutting edge traders. Many demo accounts are boundless, so not time-limited.

Segments Every Strategy Needs

Regardless of whether you're after robotized day trading strategies or tenderfoot and propelled strategies, you'll have to consider three basic parts; volatility, liquidity, and volume. In case you're to bring in money on little value developments, picking the correct stock is crucial. These three components will assist you in settling on that choice.

• Liquidity – This makes you to quickly enter and leave exchanges at an alluring and stable cost. Fluid ware strategies, for instance, will concentrate on gold, raw petroleum, and flammable gas.

• Volatility – This reveal to you your latent capacity benefit run. The digital currency market is one such model notable for high volatility.

• Volume –For day traders, this is otherwise called 'average day by day trading volume.' High volume lets you know there's critical enthusiasm forthe advantage or security. Expansion in volume is as often as possible an indicator a value hop either up or down, is quick drawing closer.

The breaking point Your Losses

At the point when you exchange on edge, you are progressively powerless against sharp value developments. Indeed, this implies the potential for more noteworthy benefit, yet it likewise implies the chance of huge misfortunes. For long positions, you can put it underneath an ongoing low. You can likewise make it dependent on volatility.

One mainstream strategy is to set up two stop-misfortunes. Initially, you put in a physical stop-misfortune request at a particular value level. Furthermore, you make a psychological stop-misfortune.

Day Trading Vs Swing Trading

Most companies in the financial markets are familiar with the different schedules that traders might have in the day to day lives so all stocks in the market are categorized according to their traders.

Traders are grouped into two categories:

• swing traders

• day traders

Swing Traders are those who buy stocks that are not fast perishable and therefore stay on the market longer.

Day Traders are in the market for something fast-moving and has a high volatility rate.

This distinction makes the different types of trading applicable to those inthe market. How to identify what stocks are suitable for day trading or swing trading is reliant on the information gotten from the different platforms.

Different website platforms are perfect for this dissemination of information as they are regularly updated and get direct information from those companies and big investors.

There is also a stark financial difference between day

trading and swing trading, and all these niches are analyzed.

Day trading vs swing trading

Just when you thought you were getting a grip on day trading; youdiscover that there is another type of trading. Swing trading is another formof trading that is undertaken by people who have not as much time as the day traders.

Similarities

While there are more stark contrasts, there are also a few similaritiesbetween these two modes:

• Day trading and swing trading are easily tracked and charted on a regular basis. Their activity on the market is manageable, and statistics are well documented regularly.

• There is always a possibility for huge profits based on the stockiest onthe market. When the stockist's graph has been on a constant rise, both day and swing traders are bound to reap heavily from it.

• There is no limit to the number of stocks. However, you will need tostick to the max dollar stop-loss rule. Both types of trading allow for the purchase of the stocks that are viable, and this is essential as they use different time frames to track.

• Both of these types of trading can be done on the same platforms, and the transactions remain the same.

• There is a real-time opportunity to keep track of the charting of your stock performance at will in both day and swing trading. There are the limits and timers that can be set by the trader to go off at the time of analysis.

Differences

Like said, all traders are grouped into two categories: swing traders andday traders.

• Day trading is for people who are impulsive and have a high level of discipline. Swing traders tend to be more cautious and take a long-timemaking decision hence the amount of time they use.

• Day trading is based mostly on making profits unlike swing trading that is done so as to identify swings in stocks and occurrences in the forex market over a period of time.

- When it comes to risks, day trading carries the most. Day traders, therefore, have to invest a lot of time in the markets due to the longevity of their stocks. Swing trading only carries the risk of having the amount out on the market for long.

- Day trading can be drawn back with a power outage while swing trading will carry on even after the power is back. Therefore, one should constantly have backup internet access or an alternative form of communication on theirstocks.

- Day trading is full time while swing trading doesn't have to be.

- Day trading rarely works with high-value stocks and focuses more on small and retail companies while swing trading mostly stocks belonging to corporate companies.

- A swing trader is able to concentrate on his own personal off time and probably strengthen his trading skills as opposed to a day trader. The day trader is always rushing to make as much profit from the maximum numberof stocks he purchased to hone his skills.

- Swing traders stand to lose out in case of a market crash than day traders are done with everything at the end of the day. This takes a lot of faith in thattheir stocks will payout and not burn out.

Strategies used in Swing Trading

Swing trading comes with different opportunities and also frequent scares. These trades are made in shaky markets, and many times the market can crash with all those dollars invested in it.

Its advantage is that it uses longer time frames to track; therefore, one can manage a full-time job as opposed to the shorter time frames on day trading. So, to avoid any pitfalls, one is advised to try it on a demo account first whilelearning the ropes. In swing trading, there's no need to keep worrying about the trades that you made. The long-time frame allows you to easily pursue other things as you wait to conduct your trade. Such a trade is very convenient since it gives room for flexibility. You would like a trade that gives you freedom. You find that you do not need to keep worrying about themoves that you make since you feel secure in your deals. As a trader, you would like to engage in a deal that grants you your freedom. You want to be at a point where you can carry out your other activities as you keep trading.In this case, swing trading will act as a side job that earns you an income.You get to do other things as you conduct swing trading. It is more likekilling two birds with one stone.

Swing trading is also best experienced once one has mastered the art of money management so that you can project your profits wisely. This advanced time on the market will help you identify the patterns in the stocks, and this will improve your decision-making ability. In any investment business, the management of money matters a lot. We have had some businesses start out really well and ended up failing. You will be amused that they do not fail due to the lack of a good strategy. Instead, they fail due to poor management of finances. Any business that looks forward to making more profits, as the years advance, needs to look at how they manage their finances keenly. We have heard of cases where businesses started out well only to end up failing before making bigger strides. Money laundering has affected many businesses to the point of closure. Once you know how to engage in swing trading, ensure that you manage your finances. This will ensure that you make better decisions while carrying out various trades. With a good money management strategy, it gets easier to make progress in swing trading. You find that you will easily double your profits with this strategy.

Due to the longer time frames, have a reliable mode of communication as one is bound to forget to make moves on the market, thus ending up withhuge losses. Timing is important in all the business deals that you engage in.

The interesting thing about most motivational talks is how they insist on proper time management. You have probably come across some people that would prefer you to waste their money but not their time. The importance of time lies in the impact that it has on an individual. The time factor is also necessary while conducting various trades. Ensure that you are keen on the decisions that you make.

For instance, with the long durations in which the trades are carried out, you may forget the time you were required to trade. You find that you have a lot going on and keeping certain dates becomes a challenge. To avoid this, you can set a reminder on when you need to trade.

At times, this will require that you are disciplined in carrying out your various activities. The decisions that you make, no matter how small, have a big impact in your possibility of succeeding. Utilizing this strategy will help you a lot while trading options. It ensures that you are disciplined in keeping time and you trade in moments when you can get a big profit.

Observe the trends in the market and steer clear of trading with the trend. This is because its longevity might be questionable and therefore having a stock that phased out while you were not tracking it is detrimental. Avoid trading against the most appealing trend and exercise caution by withholding yourself. As a trader, you need to be keen on how the market moves. You cannot achieve success in a certain area unless you fully understand what it entails. As an individual intending to engage in swing trading, one of the beststrategies that you can utilize is knowing how the market operates. You will be surprised by the power of having information. In the world that we currently live in, ignorance will cost you a lot. Nowadays, information is readily available to us that one has no excuse not to learn.

In this era of trading, on the Internet you can easily

get all the informationyou want by conducting a simple search. We also have numerous resourceson hand to help us acquire the information we would like. With the many resources, we certainly have no excuse for not having the knowledge weneed. We are also inundated with so much information that we can never completely complete learning about everything. New news come out every day and we can't stop it. Having a positive attitude towards learning and seeing the impact it will have on conducting swing exchanges allows us to improve our strategy every day.

Swing trading allows for different skill sets in the trading as it takes a while for the stocks to exit the market. During this time, the beginner can go over whatever steps he would have forgotten in order to fortify his trading process. Asides from knowledge, we need to gain skills that help us inconducting different trades. These skills make the trading process easier. The difference between the people who succeed at certain things, and those that fail lies in the extra mile that they are willing to take. How hungry are you forsuccess? What extra miles are you willing to make to get to a place that you would like to be? Your response to these questions can tell a lot about the kind of individual that you are. You find that successful people tend to be driven by their ambitions.

This does not only apply in other aspects of life, but it is also applicablein swing trading. There are many decisions that you will make, that will influence your general outcome. To become a good trader, you will have to come up with some tactics and strategies that make the trades manageable. Some people tend to view it as a complex thing, yet it is very easy to come upwith tactics and strategies. The only thing that you will need is having adequate knowledge of how swing trading operates. Once you have theinformation, it is easy to come up with the strategies.

Trading OrderTypes

Investors are utilizing a broker to buy or sell an asset utilizing their option of order form. They initiate an order once an investor has decided to buy or sell an asset. The order gives guidance to the broker regarding how to proceed.

Commercial securities are usually traded through a mechanism of bid/ask.A buyer is willing in paying the price of selling must be present to sell is meant by this.

There needs to be a ready seller to offer as the price of the buyer to purchase. No deal happens when a buyer is there and the seller isalso there. The offer is the highest price advertised that someone is ready for asset pay, and the request is the lowest price advertised at which someone is ready to asset sell. The changes in the bid and the ask are constant, as each offer and bid represent some order.

The rates can change when commands are filled out. E.g., if a 25.25 bid isthere and another bid of 25.26, the next highest bid is 25.25 when all 25.26 orders have been completed. This process of bid / ask is a key to remember when an order is placed, as the selected order type will affect the price at which filled the trade, when it is going to be filled out, or whether it is going to filled out at all.

Types of Orders

Orders are taken in most markets by the individual as well as institutional investors. Mostly by broker-dealers, individuals trade that requires to place many types of orders when doing business. Markets facilitate various types oforders which provide some discretion to invest when planning a trade.

Some basic types of order are as follows:

A market order shall instruct the brokerage in order completion at the price available. Market orders have no fixed demand and are usually performed on all occasions when there is little competition in the exchange. Market orders are used typically when the trader wants quickly the trades in or out and the price is not the concern they are getting.

The brokerage is instructed by the order cap to acquire at or less than a defined amount, the security. Limit orders make sure a customer just pays a certain security purchasing price. Limit orders may remain effective till executed, expired, or canceled.

A broker is instructed by the sell limit order to sell at a price above the price currently, the asset.

Such form of order is used for long positions to have gains as the price rises higher since purchasing. The brokerage is instructed by the order of sell stop to sell if the asset is or reaches at a price less than the price currently. A buy order stop may tell the dealer to acquire an asset until it hits a level abovethe amount currently.

A market order is the stop order meaning that once

triggered it can take any price or order of stop limit it can be and it can be only executed within a given limit (price range) after triggering.

Day order shall be conducted on the same business day on which theorder is setted up.

An order remains effective until it is cancelled.

If the order isn't a day order, the trader sets typically the order expiration.Trade results are affected by these kinds of orders. For example, a buylimit placed at a price lower than the asset is currently trading can give abetter price to the trader if it decreases the asset in value (in comparison tobuying it now). But waiting for the price to drop to the expected limit impliesthat, in the event that the price does not reach the limit value, the trader may
miss the opportunity to open the trade.

One type of order is no better than the other, it is important to select the right one for you're trading style and according to the market you are trading in.

Example of Order Usage for a Stock Trade. A trader must think abouthow to buy a stock and under what conditions he will avoid a loss maximise aprofit. This means that 3 orders can potentially be entered at the start of the trade: one to enter, one to control the risk if the price does not move as expected (stop-loss), and the order to close the trade if the price moves in the expected direction. An investor or trader may not place their closing orders atthe same time they start the trade, but must know how to exit (with a profit / loss) by closing the trade, both technically and strategically.

If a trader decides to buy AAPL (Apple Inc.). Orders must be placed keeping risks under control but which can ensure a profit.

Based on the alert from a technical indicator, we place a commercialorder for the purchase of the product at $ 124.15. The order will reach $ 124.17. The difference between the purchase and execution set price is known as slippage. You don't have to bet more than 7 percent on the product as stop loss, so the sales order for $ 115.48, 7% less. This is to get apredictable loss without risking too much.

Based on the strategy, the expected gain is 21%, which implies that the ratio is three times the stop loss. This is a strong risk / reward ratio. Therefore, the sell order limit is set at $ 150.25 which is 21% higher than the entry price.

First, an order of selling will be there, by which the trade will be closed. In this scenario, the price first reaches the limit of selling, results in a profit of21% for the trader.

Market Order Definition

An investor's bidis an order of market –made usually through a brokerageor service of brokerage – for buying or selling a stock at the price best available in the present market. The most reliable and fastest way of entering or exiting a trade, it is considered widely and gives the best way to get in the trade or out of it quickly. Business orders virtually instantaneously step in for other liquid stocks large-cap. Of all the orders the basic most are considered market order. It is intended to be implemented at the existing selling price fordefense as quickly as possible. That's why other brokerages have a button of Buy / Sell trading apps.

Typically perform a business order by clicking this switch. In casesmostly market orders experience any type of order lowest commissions, sinceeither broker requires very less work.

Key Takeaways

- Market ordering is an investor's request for security buying and selling.

- Large price instruments like large-cap options, derivatives or ETFs arewell adapted.

- An order of market will be executed by the trader if he/she is ready atthe requested price to buy or at the requested price to sell.

When Market Order be Used

For securities traded in extremely high volumes like stocks of large-cap, ETFs or futures, market orders are well suited. For E-mini S&P the orders aremarket, for example a stock like Microsoft tends very quickly to fill without issue. Of stocks with weak floats or limited total regular value, this is a different matter. As such stocks are traded thinly, the distribution of the asking bid appears to be large. Due to this, market orders are sometimes slowly filled for securities like these, and at prices unexpected often which leads to significant trading costs.

Slippage of Market Order

It implies that if a dealer wants to fulfill a trading offer, the seller is ableto purchase at the selling price or sold at the price of the bid. Thus, themarket order executing guy leaves the asked bid spread immediately.

For reasons like this, it is the best idea sometimes to take a close look at the spread of the asked bid before an order of the market is placed– especiallyfor securities traded thinly. Failure of doing so could incur very large costs. Itis doubly relevant to the individuals also who regularly deal, or whatever utilizes an electronic training program.

Market Order Vs Limit Order

The basic most buying and selling trades are market orders. Also, on the different side, limit orders allow the investors more extra price control of bid price or price of sale. It is achieved by specifying a maximum reasonable value of the sales price or an appropriate minimum acceptable price of sale.

The ideal is the Limit orders for trading thinly traded

stocks, are volatile highly or have larger asked bid spreads.

Market Order Example of Real World

Assume the asked bid production costs for Excellent Industries shares are respectively 18.50 dollars and 20 dollars, with hundred shares available on request. If an order is placed by the trader for buying 500 shares on the market, at 20 dollars the first hundred will execute.

Nonetheless, the upcoming 400 fill up the upcoming 400 securities at the highest selling price for sales. If traded the stock very thinly, the upcoming 400 shares could be executed around 22 dollars or greater. This is exactlywhy the usage of limit limits for such forms of shares is a smart idea. The market orders trade-off filled at a dictated market price in opposition to restricting or stopping orders which give more control to traders. Sometimes the use of market orders may result in unintended or significant costs in someof the cases.

Definition of Limit Order

The most basic of all orders is considered market order. It is intended to be implemented at the existing selling price for a defense as quickly as possible. That's why other brokerages have Buy / Sell button trading apps. Typically perform a business order by clicking this switch. In cases mostly the order of market least commission of any type of order is incurred since either broker requires very less work.

AdditionalFinancial Tools

There are numerous financial instruments available. A financial instrument signifies a type of contract between two parties. It can be defined as a document that represents a liability to one party and an asset to another. All financial instruments can be legally enforced and contain monetary value. These financial instruments can be created, traded, and even modified.

Financial instruments can be documents or contracts. Contract documents include stocks, bonds, options, and future. However, they can broadly be classified as either derivative instruments or cash instruments. Derivatives are instrumenting whose value is derived from the characteristics and value of the underlying instrument. Cash instruments derive their value entirely from the markets. A good example of a cash instrument is a stock or share. These are very easy to liquidate or transfer.

There are plenty of other classifications depending on the type, asset classand so on. For instance, debt instruments can be classified as either long-term or short-term debts. Others such as Forex-based instruments are in a class of their own.

Stocks

Stocks are the most common type of security that you are likely to come across. These are traded at the stock market which is a secondary market. Owners or holders of stocks usually trade with willing buyers on a regular basis at the stock exchange. On most occasions, if not all, you will be buying or trading in stocks with other interested participants but not the parent company.

Every stock comes with a quote. This quote is never fixed but varies depending on a number of factors. Prices are not the only information provided. We also have other information available relating to stocks. For instance, traders are interested in volumes traded as the volume is a great indicator of liquidity.

The prices of stocks are often determined through an auction process at the stock exchange. Buyers and sellers basically place bids and offer and when they coincide a sale is concluded. If you wish to buy stocks you will visit your broker who will place bids on your behalf. Alternatively, you can open an online account and do so via a trading platform. Most transactions have moved online making it easier and more convenient to trade in stocks and shares.

There are different kinds of orders when it comes to the stock market. Forinstance, we have limit orders and market orders. A market order is where a client uses an online platform or instructs a broker to sell or buy stocks at the best price possible. Market orders never guarantee the price that you want butyou will almost certainly get the number of shares desired.

Introduction to Limit Orders

A limit order refers to a set price that will be used to sell or purchase a security or other financial asset. When an investor uses a limit order, thenthey get to determine the price at which securities are sold or bought. This is completely different from market orders because in this case, a sale or buy order will only execute when the limit order is attained.

Example

Take the example where an investor wants to purchase XYZ stock at $60.The current price of XYZ stock is $62 so the limit order is set at the $60price. XYZ stocks will be purchased once this price is attained. The price may fluctuate either way but no purchase is made until the price of $60 is attained. The order is executed until the desired number of shares is purchased.

Now assume that the investor wishes to sell the same XYZ stock at $63. A limit order of that amount will be set. Once this price is reached then the order is executed and the stock is sold. This is how effective and powerful the limit order is.

This order executes only when the set price is attained. It is completely different to a market order. Market orders tend to execute at prevailing market conditions. Traders prefer to limit orders because of their precision. These orders are especially useful in a volatile market. Limit orders provide more control over the process of purchasing and selling stocks.

How to Apply for Limit Orders

Limit orders are mainly used when certain market conditions are prevalent. Think about situations when a particular stock is trading at ranges between $60 and $70. This is considered an extremely volatile stock and the limit order would come in handy in such a market. Anyone using market order will be at a disadvantage because they will not be able to control the buying price.

Limit orders are also useful in situations where the trader is preoccupied and unable to keep track of the markets. The orders will protect his interests and ensure that he remains in control of buying or selling price. It is also possible to have limit orders left open but with a distinct expiration date.

Apart from limit and market orders, we also have stop orders. There are clear differences between all these different orders. All these orders areissued to the broker who will execute them as directed. The important part to note is that both limit and stop orders oppose market orders. Instead of letting the market determine the price, it is the trader who determines their sell orbuy price.

Limit order simply means an all or none order. In this instance, when you place an order, it will only be fulfilled if you receive the entire amount of shares that you desire. For instance, if you wish to purchase 500 shares of stock ABC, then this AON or all-or-none order will only be fulfilled if the 500 shares are available.

If the supply falls short, then the order will not be fulfilled.

Stop Orders

A stop order can be defined as an order placed by a trader or investor to their broker instructing them to sell or purchase certain security such asstocks when a certain price is exceeded.

Stop orders are preferred when it is important to enter or exit a trade at a predetermined point. The main aim of this order is to lock in profits or in other cases prevent or limit losses. Should the price cross any exit or entry points, then it becomes at this point a market order.

Example

In this case, we have a trader who owns 300 shares of ABC stock. Each share costs $10 but the trader believes the share price will rise to $13 within one month's time. However, the trader does not wish to lose money should the price start falling. Therefore, the broker receives instructions to place a stop order at $9. The stop order will then initiate a market order so that shares are sold. Therefore, if the price does rise the trader will make a profit but if the price falls, the losses will be limited.

Important Points to Note

In general stop, orders are activated as soon as the price of a stock moves beyond a certain set point. There are generally two distinct types of stop orders. One is a stop order for selling and the other is for buying stocks. These orders are ideally used to lock in profits after a price increase or to limit losses on the downward trend.

Inherent Differences between Stop Orders and Limit Orders

Orders are generally issued to stockbrokers after a trade is initiated. They guide a broker on how to react to activity on the trading platform. This way, atrader is able to be more specific about how they want their trades executed. Both stop and limit orders are clear messages to the broker that a price other than the market price is what is needed. The market price is basically the price at which a stock is trading at the markets.

A limit order is generally known and visible. It can be dictated by a trader and executed as indicated.

However, a stop order is never visible in the markets. It only becomes visible as soon as it triggered. Stop orders generallyprevent risks from happening.

Stop orders matter

Stop orders are widely considered as investing in and trading strategies. They constitute an essential strategy that helps traders minimize losses while benefiting without limit on an upward trend. These orders also help with automation. When instituted, a trader will not need to regularly and consistently monitor their trades. This provides not just relief but peace of mind so that a trader can attend to other matters. Stop orders help to prevent against partial fills as well as no fills. Traders can expect their orders to be filled as desired. These are some of the reasons why stop orders are extremely crucial.

Example

In this instance, there will be a contingency placed on a preferred price or amount. You may wish to sell or buy stocks at a certain given price. Oncethis price is exceeded, then all buying or selling will stop. For instance, if youare buying shares, you may want to purchase at a price not exceeding $50. Aslong as the stock price remains at or below this price, then the order is met. But once the stock price exceeds \$50, the order will stop.

Margin trading

We also have a strategy known as margin trading. Margin refers to a loan provided by a broker for trading purposes. When you engage in margin trading, it simply means that you are purchasing stocks using borrowedfunds. The same is true when it comes to shares or stocks that do not belong to you. When you sell short, it means that you are selling shares that belongto someone else.

Both margin and short selling are popular with traders. The purpose is always to sell or buy with the aim of buying back or selling with the aim of profiting from the venture. At the same time, you will trade with the hope of returning borrowed stocks or repaying the margin loan.

Stock Indexes

We can define an index as a measure or indicator of a certain parameter. When it comes to financing, the index refers to a measure of the change in a given market. We have stocks, shares, and bonds as securities traded in the financial markets. Some of the popular indexes in the US include the S&P500 as well as the DJIA or Dow Jones Industrial Average. We also have others such as the US Aggregate Bond Index. These are often used to benchmark the performance of the US bonds and stock markets and these are measures of the US economy.

A Closer Look at Indexes

There are different indexes and each related directly to either bonds or stock markets. Also, each index has a specific calculation formula. Usually, the numeric value of an index is not as important as the relative change of theindex. The most crucial part to investors is often the total amount an indexhas fallen or risen with a period of time like 24 hours for instance.

Indexes have a base level of 1,000. However, investors and traders are often interested in the variation of the index from this base level. For instance, if the FTSE 100 has a value of 7643.50, then we can see that it is almost 8 times larger than the base level. As a trader, you need to be on the lookout for the percentage drop or rise of an index.

What Should You Invest in to Be Profitable at Day Trading

Day trading is never the same for each day. A trader that has been tradingfor a length of time that is longer than a year will find that there is never two single days that are the same. Even though there are no similarities to the day,there are still patterns to the trends. They will occur over time, but they will be hidden within a random movement of price that takes place daily.

There are five-day setups that can occur over a specific amount of days, and at least one to two will occur within one day's time frame. However, theywill not all occur in the same days' time period. Learning these trade setups will help you to exploit the potential of profit.

Context within the Patterns

Know the pattern and watching are not going to be enough for a successful day trading. These patterns will occur frequently; however, they only hold power when a specific context appears. Understand the action price in order to have a great entry in day trading. Identify when the traders are stuck, and the price will have cause to surge in a direction that is forced, meaning that the traders are selling. These setups will occur during emotionalpoints. This is when traders will feel the pain or the greed. However, there is not going to be a definite that this will occur prior to big moves and it does not mean that there will be a result of big moves. We do not have an exact knowledge of what the traders think, or if the acts will take place based on these thoughts. By watching the action of the price patterns, you will see regular occurrences. These can produce results that are similar, which can improve the chance that the trade is profitable.

Impulse Buys Create Pullback That Results in a Consolidated Breakout

Trading can begin in a move that is strongly pulled in one single direction. This will take place within 5-15 minutes once the market opens for trading. The Stock Market calls this impulse wave. The price of the stock then will pull back and then stall out. This forms the consolidation so that the price will move sideways for about 3 minutes. It must occur within animpulse wave range. The pullback or consolidation has to occur lower than the price of open. Due to the initial impulses direction, the investor will wait and experience the breakout that leaves the consolidation in the direction that is equal to the stock. Breakouts that head in the opposite direction are not traded. You want to consolidate and pull back if the price is rallied as soon asit opens. Next, you should wait for that price to be above the consolidated breakout price, and then the long trade is triggered. Consolidation must be, compared to others, small in relation to the impulse wave that is going to precede it. The pattern becomes less effective when the consolidation iscompared to the large impulse wave. During the pullback, there should be a distinct pullback, as well as impulse waves that are distinct. If they are not distinct, then the effectiveness of the pattern is less and is avoided.

This pattern can be seen throughout the trading day and can be how a trend will form. This makes it a strategy that can be utilized on most framesof time and in the market. The most power-filled moves that a market will have will take place during the open of the day, which is why catching that first hour is important. It can mean important things for your portfolio and creates large impacts with your profitability. If it occurred later in the day, then it can create smaller moves in price.

Consolidation Reversal Breakout

Impulses are not always followed by pullbacks that are small. There can be big moves that head in one direction. However, they can grow in the movement to an even bigger direction that is opposite of the original one.This is a reversal in directionality. Focus on the big moves that are most recent.

If the price dropped to $0.20 at the open, then rallies at $0.30, do not get distracted with that first drop since it will not matter anyhow. You will now have what is called an impulse for the upside. Watch for the decline in price, just a bit, and then consolidate the stock. If the consolidation breaks $0.01 then stay longer. On the reverse, you can wait for the pullback to go to the opposite for the impulse. Then you will see the impulse has a smaller pullback.

Support/Resistance Reversal

This can be horizontal lines as well as diagonal lines. They will point you in a direction that the price has been reversed for at least 2 episodes prior. This will include that starting point. You should know that the support, as well as the resistance, is not a price exactly but an area. The setup is not required to take place near the support, nor the resistance. In other words, it can take place slightly below them or above them. This informs us to be on high alert, which is based on the fact that a reversal can be coming. Because of this, we will have to sit and wait for the consolidation that is near. There is a signal for trade if the break in price is above the support that is consolidation, or below consolidation that is resistant. If this signal occurs,the price of the trade that moved one cent higher than the consolidation close to the support and fall for resistance which occurs in the pattern. Leave the trade immediately if the resistance breaks above or below the support area. Consider that the trade of breakout could be applicable.

Breakout Area Is Strong

This is a fashionable way to trade a breakout that is either above or belowthe support major area. This is, however, one of the toughest. Although the strategies above are preferred, it is beneficial to explore strategic options for special situations that can arise. Look out for a level that has pushed back the price for multiple strategies that are basic. This price will rally and then will reach 25.25 however, and then it falls. Although it performs this danceseveral times, it can struggle to break through. Once the area has tested that price three times more, there can be an assured day trades that are noticed. Suddenly the price is reaching 25.26. This can signal shifts of importance. Breakouts do not guarantee moves that are big. You may fail to produce a move that is big, and the price can break boundaries that are strategic and sparing. By making moves away from the area, you should see a significant move away from the visual that is price tested. The pattern can lose the effectiveness that will significantly become rejected by the price that is near the area. This means that you should see several rejections that have happened over multiple times.

Once the traders push the level of the price back, it becomes a pattern ofthe power, despite the level that is sent. The price of the fact is opposite in direction for multiple occasions in the past. This shows that they have a greater resolve than the opposite directions the traders are going.

How Do You Make Day Trading Your Job

If you have opened a broker account and begin to trade stocks, you arenot required to have a license. If you plan to work for a firm to trade stocks, then you will need to acquire a series 7 license. This requires a specific number of hours in a classroom and then a test that will license you as a stockbroker. In order to sell and buy stocks for others, even as your own business, you will need the license. For your own personal financial gains, you can use an online brokerage account and earn money for yourself.

Series 7 Licensing is a test that is taken after you have completed a specific number of hours for training and learning. A job that involves trading stocks, bonds, and other securities and then you will need to follow the guidelines that are set up by the SEC. These regulations require you to have Financial Industry Regulatory Authority. This requirement states that you will need stock brokers and securities licensing representative. There are several options of FINRA registrations; however, the one that is most necessary will be the General Securities Registered Representative. This will require you to complete a class and pass the test that is called a series 7 exam. There are some limited exams that can provide you with limited securities capabilities. These allow you to trade specific bonds or options. Once you pass the proper test, you will complete the license requirements. This means that you can apply for your series 7 licenses.

In order to take the test and get licensed, you will need to have anemployer sponsor you for the test. This means being sponsored by a FINRA member for the financial company service. You will need to be hired by a brokerage firm and then put through rigorous training and put you to work with a trading mentor. They will then sponsor you for the license as asecurities trader. There are not that many pre-requisites that are required to be hired as a broker however, the licensing is required once you start to trade. Once you are hired you will have an agreement that states that you are employed only until and if you pass the series 7 test. The firm will oftentimes provide you with the training that is needed or the courses that will give you the ability to pass the test.

A self-employed trader is able to trade with no licensing requirements for trading within your own account with the broker. You have to use your own money and if you can not make it a successful career then you will lose your new career. If you begin with a smaller account and then use that to learn as you go, you will be able to profitably trade prior to turning this into your full-time work. Then you can trade the day job for a profession that is full-time and profitable.

Many of the day traders are trading stocks, although it is just as popular for a day trade to trade bonds, as well as currencies or even commodities. You generally need to look for securities that have these features:

- A trade volume that is large and highly liquid.

- Bonds that are volatile. You want changes that are frequent for the price because this allows the investor to make a quick profit.

- Stocks that are known by you. You need an understanding of what that particular stock's history in price is, and various events that designate how it will react to— economic shifts or earnings reports. This is a key deciding factor. Day traders will often only trade a selected few specific stocks, developing their expertise inthe companies that they are trading. This will help them to narrow their focus so that they are not thinking too broad.

- Newsworthy stocks are a go to. News reports on a stock have a way of triggering investors to buy or sell them. As a day trader, youwill need to be educated about these events so that you can make trades that are beneficial to you.

Conclusion

Trading is, without a doubt, an effort that you need to trust. Having the confidence that you can do this will be a fuel when you need it, clear barriers when you face them, and focus on what is essential. Belief is up the educational curve.

On the opposite hand, lack of trust is often one in all the foremostdamaging aspects of the mind of traders. When the defeats arrive, how are you going to re-bound and focus? Which happens when you begin a day with two, three, or four losses? Were you going to doubt your system, trading strategy, or skill set?

Both eyes can see that lack of trust is harmful, while faith gives us a higher chance of success. While we understand it conceptually and psychologically, our actions sometimes tell a different story.

So how are we going to build confidence in trading? What can we do to make an unshakeable belief in our abilities? When we indulge in specific things, are they going to help us create a benefit base consistently?

The answer is yes, you will, without a doubt, build trust in yourself and your skills.
Knowing is just half the battle. But if with it,
you have a fighting chance.

Successful Endeavors, I'm very diligent in maintaining my cognitive assets and self-image. Having a strong self-image and a healthy mental capital balance can lead to increased results.

With that being said, what do you think it's going to do to recall your pastsuccesses? Would you believe it's going to build up your confidence or bring it down? The question is rhetorical, but I want you to start thinking more thoroughly about it.

Over the years, I've worked with thousands of investors, and one commonfeature of most of them is that they're all good at something. Chess, chess, math, fitness, banking—you name it, they're probably good at something.

We have well over 50 physicians in our schools, many of them surgeons. We've got poker stars and tournament winners who want to turn to trade. I have a few dealers on the NYSE or some big prop table, while others are high-profile trial lawyers. Scientists, developers, IT professionals, we've got them all, and the list goes on.

As a whole, most of the students who want to study forex trading are smart, probably effective in their current field, and likely good at some skill.

So how are we going to use this to build trust?

Solution A straightforward method you can use is to learn of what you're already good at. Talk of what you've been through to get there, the challengesyou've conquered, the questions you've encountered, the barriers you've crossed, how many times you weren't confident you could be good at it. And,through all that, you've been highly skilled at it.

Note the confidence you have in executing your

talent or initiative. Have you always felt the same way you do now, especially at the beginning? Contraoriented to that. But you've got there, and now you have a professionallevel of skill in it, whether it's a hobby, a sport, a career, a martial art, a musical instrument, a work or an initiative. This current knowledge and expertise could (and should) be used in our trading process.

And take a while to suppose deeply regarding what reasonably qualities and characteristics you'll had best. Talk about it until it gives you a feeling of confidence to indulge in that task and do it well. Recall this impression and add it to dealing.

Climbing Mountains, it's essential to remember that at some point in yourlife, all of you have broken through challenges, struggles, and gone above your concerns. Maybe these were low, or perhaps they were hills, but every one of them we've scaled tells us how far we've come, and what we've accomplished along the 3 Easy Ways to Develop Confidence in Trading Forex is building trust in trading When you don't have confidence in your trading system, it's the worst feeling in the world. You don't seem to have a mission, and you doubt your worth as a trader.